VISIONS OF A MEANINGFUL LIFE

VISIONS OF A MEANINGFUL LIFE

M.L. Dhawan

GIAN PUBLISHING HOUSE
DELHI-110007

GIAN PUBLISHING HOUSE
29/6, Shakti Nagar, Delhi-110007
Phone : 7213053

ISBN 81—212—0238—8

PRINTED IN INDIA

Published by Mrs. Gayatri Garg for Gian Publishing House, Delhi and Printed at Godwall Printers, Delhi.

Dedicated to :

Dr. S.R. Sharma & Sri. Harcharan Singh Josh,
Indian Council of World Affairs, Sapru House,
New Delhi

A NOTE FOR THE READERS

"Of all that is written I love only that which is written with blood. Write with blood and you will discover that blood is spirit. It is not easy to understand the blood of another. I hate the reading idle. He who knows the reader does nothing further for the reader. Another century of readers—and spirit itself will stink. That everyone is allowed to learn to read will in the long run, ruin not only writing but thinking too.

Once spirit was God, then it became man, and now it is even becoming mob. He who writes in blood and aphorisms does not want to be read, he wants to be learned by heart. In the mountains the shortest route is from peak to peak, but for that you must have long legs. Aphorisms should be peaks; and those to whom they are addressed should be big and tall of stature. The air thin and pure, danger near and the spirit full of a joyful wickedness; these things go well together. I want hobgoblins around me, for I am courageous. Courage which scares away phantoms creates hobgoblins for itself—courage wants to laugh. I no longer feel as you do, this cloud which I see under me, this blackness and heaviness I laugh at precisely this is your thunder cloud.

You look up when you desire to be exalted. And I look down because I am exalted. Who of you can at once laugh and be exalted? He who climbs upon the highest mountains laughs at all tragedies, real or imaginary. Courageous, untroubled, mocking, violent—that is what wisdom wants us to be, wisdom is woman and loves only a warrior."

Friedrich Nietzsche

The publication of a big volume could be a matter of great satisfaction and pride for a writer, since it is a clear demonstration of his all out efforts. Its size may, however, generate, some worry for the publishers. They would like that the book sells as quickly as possible. They cannot afford to wait and see for fifteen to twenty years when some one suddenly discovers the merit of a work lying in the dust and then a few editions are brought out in quick succession. A writer is generally indifferent to the profit or loss side of his work. His concernments are that the work should be published and thereafter find a large readership.

Reader

I believe that even a writer is also of lesser consequence, though he thinks that his works are important. The real person who matters in the whole "Act" is the reader. He cannot be treated casually. Books do not grapple with thc problems. It is the readers, in fact, who go through the details given in a work, and ponder over that. They may accept or reject the suggestions given therein.

A reader is not obliged to purchase a book till he is convinced that it would benefit him beyond the price he has paid. There is another dilemma of our times. He fears the prohibitive price even of a useful book. What to say of him, even the Controllers of the Public Libraries brush aside the idea of purchasing high priced books. So many of good books remain unread by the people in general. Knowledge contained therein does not spread widely. Such books fail to create that sensation which the writer had aspired. I do not recollect even a single book published in India during the last twenty five years which had fired the imagination of the readers to an extent that page of our history could have been turned. It does not imply that writers have failed or publishers did not rise to the occasion. Only readers have not moved.

My task is more intricate. I am trying to tread the unbeaten paths, wish to attack those citadels of thoughts which are no longer relevant but are still stable and appear to be well entrenched. People do not raise critical qestions against them. They prefer to live in the cages of their traditional thoughts with the hope of being all secure and for that do not wish to come out of their psychic imprisonment. They think themselves to be well fortified and thus adhere to their irrelevant past with reverence. I wish to make them realise that we happen to live in difficult times in which they should not always look for security since that is in fact fictitious. The blind guidance from the history, cultures and civilisations does not lead us very far. We have to apply our own minds and work out new guidelines. Even if we fail, that does not matter. We are even ready to face persecutions if that is so destined. We are to awaken our spirit. Our people have survived a long period of foreign suppression since they could preserve it some how. Now the same is to be strengthened and converted into an iron will to transform the present state of affairs. Polite arguments and spineless criticism would not help much.

Common Man

I pierce straight through the heart of things that touch the common man like you and me. I am not a historian who would dig into the the past and snub some rulers and leaders here and there apportioning all blame over them for our failures and defeats. I am no futurologist too who would build castles in the air. I am, of course, optimistic about future. I live in the present age ; I live with it and for it. I am a common man, a petty pensioner with no resources of comfortable living. I know my problems. Beyond it, I have no pretensions and possess a strong sense of belonging to the "category of Common man". I do not aspire to be a prophet, nor a mini prophet nor a utopian nor a leader nor a sooth sayer and nor even an astrologer. I have tried to state things with the best of my ability and understanding.

Fidelity to facts is very important to me. I am not concerned with grave matters regarding life, death, fate, existence and so on. There are many greatly illumined minds elaborating over them. With all humility, I have tried to be rational, analytical and critical to the extent it has been possible. I am conscious of my limitations. Element of objectivity is very important for a writer, but I have incidently many objectives to achieve in this short span of life that is left as my share. It is not enough that we should just demolish the decadent and outlived culture. We are to examine its present structures and raze to the ground only those of the parts which have become harmful or precarious. Let us at the same time introduce those constructs of thoughts in our life which may help it to grow and prosper. It is growth, progress and development.

A writer should be all concerned with his own age. He is living it. He experiences it from so many angles. It cannot so happen when he is studying the volumes of history. His touch with the past is always bookish and never real. He cannot physically transport himself in those times when he was not there. Every writer believes that he belongs to unusual times since his experiences of all other limes are unreal.

New Goals

It would be a great achievement if I could address myself to common men and women who are living as faceless individuals or say as shadows through the medium of this work. Here is search for new goals for them.

I would be happy if my findings are criticised ruthlessly and I am declared all wrong. That would mean that some of my readers have been provoked and they are angry. They have higher and better things to say than I could throw up. I would then take that my effort has been well rewarded. There is no mechanistic formula that may provide the details as to how the ascendancy of a common man is possible. Here is just an effort to awaken some of his latent capacities. Real life lies in battling against those odds which choke it in general. This was known to the mankind even many thousands years ago. As an idea it holds water even today.

It is a prophetic way to state that the individual can move the Heavens. He can do this and that. This is all humbug in the practical sense of the term. All his potentialities are theoretical. Even many of his possibilities appear to be imaginary. His conditions are seldom that satisfactory where his capacities could be best discovered. Generally he lacks the means of realising his 'best self' but it is not always so. Since time immemorial he had suffered in silence. He could have been exterminated if it had bcen in the interest of the powerful. He has of course paid very heavy price merely for his biological existence till date and now for living 'effectively' he shall have to suffer still more. He may be crushed in the process of the fierce struggles and that too without leaving a trace. There may be many who would die heroically without ever being sung, remembered. This state of affairs would perhaps continue unmitigated in the foreseeable history.

Reader's Responsibilities

Every literate person can be a reader but in recent times serious readership has been reduced to bare minimum. There are very few who equip themselves in the art of reading. In the beginning it is difficult to read effectively but gradually it becomes a privilege for an individual.

Whatever may be the caste or class or profession or even nationality of the reader he is under no obligation of a writer. The former can be at times a more qualified person than that of the latter. It, however, goes without saying that a writer shall have to be a purposeful reader prior to wielding his own pen. He can ill afford to take his studies lightly.

Qualified readers and almost all writers have no serious respect for the printed word. Their own minds are fairly developed. They exercise them and draw their own conclusions. Generally whatever a writer has described would be conveyed to the readers as he desires, but whatever he thinks or imagines or wishes or aspires, the readers should understand, depends upon his art of communication.

A reader's critical faculty should always be at work. He is not expected to take things for granted. A casual reader is inconsequential. He has all respects for the printed word. He takes the writer as a very serious personality. He believes the statements and ideas contained in a book as if these are all truths. With the increasing literacy and declining seriousness such readership is multiplying.

The so-called educated people have neither time nor patience to read books beyond their professional need. They are concerned only with such works that help them to grow in terms of their careers. In general illumination of mind is considered a futile exercise since it does not help the individual materially. It is not easily saleable. There are no buyers of it.

This is an age in which swindling of money has become very important. All out efforts are being made by the people around for acquiring wealth and higher standards of livings. In the process the standard of thinking has pathetically fallen. Minds do not transcend of their own. Long and consistent efforts are to be made for it. Unfortunately such advice is no longer coming from those who really matter in the new world order.

There is another dilemma. I am worried about the plight of our young readers. How much should they read since the human knowledge is exploding at a terrific speed ? How much would they be able to stretch their time ? The life span of an individual is ultimately limited. His faculties are also limited, but awaiting him is growing enormously.

CONTENTS

1

VISIONS OF A MEANINGFUL LIFE : INTRODUCTION

"We face a period of hard new thinking on the political structure of society and on the position and the role of the individual in it. What we have so far is new pluralism, a new society of organisations. What we need is a new individualism a new responsibility."

Peter F. Drucker

As soon as an individual sees the light of the day, so many forces take charge of his development. To mention only a few, these are parentage, family, religion, race, place of birth, and many other conditions that surround him. Genetics had its own role to play. He is formed and deformed in so many ways before the normal efforts for his formal education are initiated.

Common Man

He is too small in the scheme of things. Outwardly he appears to be all quiet, sober, and meditative. He is of course not a dud. Even if he has not learnt much from home and schools, life has been his alma-mater. It must have taught him at least how to survive. At times he is a live-wire too. He may not be able to explain the peculiar intricacies of modern life but certainly experiences its nefarious implications. He goes to the market. He knows how the prices of the articles he needs are shooting up. Other things apart, that is enough to make him feel the hardness of times in which he is living. Apparently he does not react, but he asks himself what has gone wrong. He asks others around as to what is happening.

Even if he is a bit literate he does not read books. He is not conversant with the details of news and views given in different daily and weekly newspapers, journals and magazines. He, of course, listens to a few Radio and TV programmes. Here he is explained about the achievements of the ruling parties and their leaders. Such means of communication would not help him to know why the material side of his life is becoming more and more difficult. He may not be able to stretch his arguments but always feels threatened or destabilised by those forces that do not help him to overcome his poverty.

In the process he may be decimated but he is still against waging life and death struggle against the existing political and administrative organisations. To him peace is always precious. With all frustrations he has not given up. If he is thoughtful in his approach, he believes that peaceful means should be evolved for achieving revolutionary ends. He needs more electricity, more water, more fertilisers, better seeds, more food, more clothes, more houses, more schools, more hospitals, more industries, more roads, more factories, more jobs, more work and above all less number of children, less police stations, less liquor shops, less murders, less rapes no invasions from outside, no civil war inside and at the top of all no unemployment. All this cannot be achieved over night and for that lot of infrastructure is to be built up first.

Historically speaking he has lived in a world in which the ideological threads of the socio-economic system were never tied up. He has no coherent set of values which could have pushed him forward for overcoming his backwardness. He has also made no outstanding efforts in shaping himself. He has not even challenged those forces unleashed by others to suppress him. He is what he has been made by the conditions under which he has been destined to grow.

It is very important that the individual should be himself. He should not feel elated on being hailed as a Gandhian or a Marxist or a Nehruite or something else. A mere act of aiming at something higher does not make him great. He must know what he stands for. Instead of being a blind or semi-blind follower of a leader or a dud disciple of some saint, he should be himself. He must feel that he is also making history.

He is not just to spend his life rather live his times. He should try to collect all his physical, intellectual, moral and spiritual strength to the extent it is possible. That would help him to become self-reliant to the degree it is possible. He is to learn not to depend upon others. Well, if he does not help himself, others would not come to oblige him. In general he has still to learn that he matters. He can scrabble his way through. He has certain capacities which are lying undiscovered. That would ultimately transform his conditions.

He is to be trained for looking up. He is to be committed for searching something better and higher. He should exercise his own mind to thrash out the problems confronting him. Once inherent possibilities are understood by him, he would push his way througth. He must bear in mind that he is on a long and sacred pilgrimage of life. It is a rare opportunity.

Man is for all purposes, a finite animal. His reality is far less than his possibility. That latter is far less t an his potentiality. He must try to climb from reality to possibility, to potentiality. This is his solemn duty. It is not enough, that he may boast of the gift of his intelligence, he must nurture it further, apply it and defend it.

Many Sufi Saints and Vedantins have asserted the infinite potential of man. Well, we have no means to prove it all beyond doubt. It can, however, be safely said that his potential is enormous. He uses only a fraction of it and rest of it goes waste and life reaches full stop. As such, his achievements are always far less than those of the potentialities he has.

The difficulty with the common man is that he does not investigate in himself. He lives on borrowed knowledge which does not carry him too far. Over it, he becomes the victim of routinised life and that too robs his initiative. It is only the deadly crash of life that produces an effective personality out of him since otherwise he remains something inconsequential.

Whatever may be the social status of a particular individual he must bear in mind that he matters. It is to be ensured that others do not take him casually. He has some merit. Even if, he lives lowly and leads a very nominal life apparently or may appear to be engaged in realising some little known purpose in life he deserves respect and affection from all around.

I have come across many unknown people whose activities are never reported in the press but they are engaged in certain ennobling pursuits. They are quietly moving from one possibility to another. Sharks of publicity just ignore them for reasons best known to them.

Biology

The role of Biology is very important in determining the futurity of an individual, his physical structure, complexion and even intelligence. It is true that as a man, he is not made to crawl. He is required to stand up. He is capable of growing physically, intellectually, morally and so on. Since the process of his further growth continues even after his emergence as a man on this earth, so he cannot be hailed as something created in all finality. We do not know as to how the future course of his evolution would unfold. It is quite possible that better animals than the present man, may roam about on this earth in some distant times, but that should not scare our generation. We are concerned with the human material as it is, think and work over its present and future. Physically speaking, man is frail as his ancestors used to be, he has a very short span of life as compared to a few other animals.

Opportunity

No great opportunity has ever come in the way of a common man otherwise he would not have remained enlisted in this category. If a creeper could grow up and up say by the support of a delicate thread, man is a superior species. There is another view that he has made no serious efforts to scrutinise and understand his potential. He is considered take aware that he is not a speck of dust but at the same time he believes odds are heavy and against him. He is intersected and interwoven by innumerable hardships in earning his life. He often gets lost in the efforts of earning two square meals and just sets aside the real purpose of his journey from birth to death. Well, he can not walk out of his life so long as he is alive. It has been noticed that time comes when his zeal to live begins to enervate but still he drags on.

Religious Spirit

He may be a peasant, a worker, a teacher, a clerk or absorbed in some other petty profession. Where can he go beyond the immediate worlds of his family ? His village ? His profession ? His caste ? His community ? His region ? The spirituality in whatever form he has inherited comes to his rescue more especially when he is frustrated on account of his defeats. There is an element of faith in him which sustains him since it suggests to him that there is an "unquenchable spark of divinity" in each one of us. This is to be fanned for becoming "a flame of spiritual realisation". Here he is face to face with the Almighty. He integrates himself with the cosmos. At this stage the painful realities of his life remain far behind. Well at the face of it, we treat a big statement, but it lends him a lot of psychic support.

The instinct of self-preservation is another reason which helps animals to survive. Man is no exception. He submits to live in this greedy, cruel, crazy, cowardly and stupid world. The will to survive has always been the first priority awaiting him to attend to. We have to improve upon, it. It is not enough that he should cling to his life passionately, he must make it meaningful. He must live as a force to be reckoned with. He must defend his atom of sovereignty.

Man is the only animal known till date who could grasp certain intricate secrets of nature. His task is not yet over. He is still engaged in this pursuit. He is transforming the world in the light of his new learning and fresh experiences. He has continuously been absorbing influences without fully being aware of them all. Whether there is some purpose in the scheme of cosmos or not, it is yet to be established by the scientists, but the leaders of all religions, ideologies and philosophies assert that there is certainly some objective of human life. It is, therefore, not to be taken lightly.

Not All Static

It generally appears as if common man has compromised with his humble existence. In the words of Emerson he is "a god in ruins". There could be occasions when he has certain strong desires, but his level of their achievement is low. So now he is reconciled with the belief that "to be great is simply to be misunderstood" otherwise he has all those intrinsic qualities that should help him to come up. He is annonymous, something to be unseen, unnoticed, and unwatched, still he is a human being not just a numeral in a book of statistics. "If a man", wrote Coleridge, "is not rising upwards to be an angel, depend upon it, he is sinking downwards to be a devil. He cannot stop at the beast. The most savage of man are not beasts, they are worse, a great deal worse''.

Trials

The merit of an individual lies in the fact that if there is tyranny all around, he must stand up against it. If there is an indiscipline and disorder, he is to take up the cudgels for restoring order and peace. No compromise on those essentials which make life purposeful and hopeful. His overall approach should be positive and constructive. He is to so weave his thinking that petty things of life do not come in to offset him.

He is not required to waste his talent and energies in gnashing teeth over those developments which he does not approve. All out efforts are to made to locate them and then take suitable remedial steps to the extent possible.

He is not expected to spend his precious time in long and idle prayers. There are people around who are all involved in such a work. Each and every moment of life is very important to him. He needs not ask others to do those things which he himself is unable to do.

Nothing spectacular can be achieved by marching on the beaten paths. Institutions may be set up that may help him to locate his possibilities denovo in the changing conditions. It is not less risky than walking on the razor's edge even for those who are considered highly qualified. Inspiring millions and millions for it would be still more difficult.

Whether he is exceptionally talented or not, he should try to be humble and graceful in his day to day life. His real gifts would not remain long undiscovered if he also tries to ask himself as to what best can be done by him.

In the battle of life there are almost equal possibilities of success and failure. If he succeeds, purpose of his life stands realised. If he fails, the world may see no merit in his struggle but he knows his efforts and therein also lies the transformation of his personality to a considerable degree.

2

LIMITATIONS

"We are great fools. "He has spent life in idleness". We say "I have done nothing today". What have you lived? That is not only the fundamental but the most illustrious of your occupation. "If I had been placed in a position to mangage great affairs, I would have shown what I could do." Have you been able to think out and manage your own life ? You have done greatest task of all."

Motaingue

The winds of modernisation are blowing around common man. He cannot remain all unaffected. A constitutional right to vote for electing his governmet comes in his way after every four five years. He then feels elated for being acknowledged when the electioneering campaigns are in full swing. He physically looks at those who are known as rulers or leaders and about whom he reads in the press hears over radio and watches them on TV. He is highly impressed by their physical presence in his midst since he is aware of them as omnipotents who can make or mar his life. He knows that they are not his relatives and friends. They have come to seek his small support for acquiring the legitimacy of their holding on the political power over him. He is a drop in the ocean but political leaders are to collect those drops for converting them into oceans of force in which they navigate. Common man understands it thoroughly well that he is of no consequence. Even a tiny ant can harm his interests since he has been incapacitated by the cruelty of times. As a helpless creature he tries to be friendly with all, fearing others are monsters around. He is aware of their nuisance value, and he is conscious that he is not in a position to hit back.

Ruling Party

The protagonists of the ruling party laud their achievements in all the fields. It is impressed upon common man that there has been unprecedented increase in food production over the years. The threats created by droughts and famines have long been wiped out. There has been substantial progress in vast and expanding areas of science and technology also. India is no longer an agricultural country. It has now acquired a commendable position even amongst the industrial nations. Common man is also assured of more water for agriculture, more electricity, diesel, more industries, more machines, more fertilisers, better seeds, more jobs, more schools, more houses, more hospitals and so on. It is also pledged time and again that the very face of the country would soon be transformed through rapid all-round economic developmenl. He is nowhere impressed that he shall have to work hard. Who would produce all these things for him ? He knows the party's members thoroughly well. He is aware of their past performances. The Heavens would not come to his rescue. So he applies his sixth sense and soon realises that much would not change. His lot is not destined to look up. He transports himself to the imaginary world of fate. It shapes his will, to act, but helps in the conditioning of his mind to adjust with those situations which cannot be turned favourable to him.

Opposition Parties

He just tries to know more about the actual state of affairs. He happens to meet even those who are not favourably disposed towards the Ruling Party. The opposition Parties highlight the vices, crimes, weaknesses and other failures of the party in power. They complain that government is corrupt right from the bottom to the top. Over the years, there has been biting price rise of those articles that are used by the people, in general. These spokesmen of opposition try to pose themselves as if they are future Messiahs. This is all nonsense. The truth is that on previous occasions they were defeated at the polls. They wish to seize power some how. They ask questions: Did rulers ever come out with programmes to guarantee full employment ? Did they ever suggest improvement in social lives of the people ? Did they ever fight against dowry system ? or Bride Burning? Did they ever crusade against deforestation ? No. No. No. Q.E.D. The rulers are therefore declared unsuccessful. Opposition should thus be given opportunity to set the things right. Here common man is dismayed. He asks a few questions. Did the leaders of opposition ever appeal to the society to increase production ? Did they ever throw up positive suggestions in the fields of education. Agriculture ? Industries ? Foreign Policy ? The truth is that our opposition parties are as good or bad as our rulers. They are all chips of the same block. Their principal motive is to be in power or seize it.

Protests

Under the circumstances common man is lying unnerved. He has become almost indifferent to all that is said or done. He has lost all hopes. He is no longer anxious to join agitations or protest marches. He is conscious that such gimmicks would not produce the required fruit. There are, of course, a few professional processionists in all the big cities. They are available on reasonable payments. Their services can be hired if some procession is to be organised by some party. They would raise slogans as desired by those who have met the expenses. In the given conditions common people ridicule those who happen to proceed on "Hunger Strikes" or "Dharnas," or "Pen down strikes" or something else for some cause. Just as Gandhian cap has spent its respectability, same is the fate of many Gandhian methods of protests.

Gandhian Norm

It is high time that common people should coordinate their feelings, emotions, sense impressions, perceptions and experiences. All this would help them to draw their own conclusions for the issues confronting them. Political imagination coupled with yearnings to help others who are needy is not the prerogative of the so-called "cultured people". Gandhi Ji had had correctly pointed out "Recall the face of the poorest and weakest man, whom you may have seen, and ask yourself, if the step you contemplate is going to be of any use to him; will he gain anything by it." We all can make use of this formulation. This is a sure test for determining the quality of an activity. It is also free from the constraints of so-called higher learning and ideological confusion.

History

Common man quietly watches how history is being unfolded and power being exercised by those who could manipulate. Instinctively being peaceful he respects the prevailing political and administrative system. We may call him a moderate or a conservative, he is a respector of the established norms of life. He is not in favour of quick changes. He submits even to the rotten traditions of the past, when there is no justification to uphold them. He feels all secure by walking over the beaten paths. He fears that if he adopts a different approach, from that which is normally expected of him, he may set wrong trends and generate chaotic situations. Circumstances might then go out of control and he would not be in a position to contain them. What is settled by time old practices is considered all safe by him. Well, it goes without saying that, if set procedures are strictly adhered to, the possibilities of encountering perils are minimized, but chances of progress are also affected.

Cause and Effect

It is complained that common man is not hard working. He is wedded to passivity. He has worked out a style of life which is convenient and serves the purpose of living at low key. So he is not actively involved in grappling with issues. This gradually enervates his personality. The physical weakness caused by poor diet and sorrowful environment and over it by mental backwardness on account of illiteracy or poor quality of education if at all received, have all resulted in the creation of negative way of his life and that is why it appears as if he exists in the state of "suspended animation". Our efforts should be directed to the end that we get him out of it.

He has neither physical nor financial, nor political nor

intellectual and nor even social power to assert his identity. He has been made to live in this manner for such a long time that now he scorns all forms of power that operate around him. Time has come for his rise and assertion. For that he shall have to seize power of some kind. It is then to be used for wresting those benefits that have not come to his share so far. This is a real issue. Once some form of power is seized, it would then be used for consolidating his position. Its present use, he finds, is arbitrary and autocratic. It is processes are to be reversed and its constructive application is to be set in motion.

Higher Objectives

Search for higher values and then by adapting himself to them would help out a common man to proceed on in a right direction. Here he is not to restrict himself to thinking part only rather grapple with the issues intelligently and courageously.

The individual may carefully plan and then act boldly to make some headway. He may win, but there is no guarantee.

It is true that in our times there has been unprecedented increase of knowledge in all the fields that concern man. It is undoubtedly some thing very important. We find so many opportunities are opened to us and at the same time perils are mounting. Where the solutions of certain problems are in sight but the means to reach them are found through thorny lanes. Our vision has blurrings and thereby the possibilities of clear thinking have reduced. He is, therefore, advised not to lose courage. It is his asset to a very great extent. He must get a feel that he is not disappointed on any score and displays the adequate stamina to live up to all hardships. If he is facing heavy odds, he should not submit on account of real or imaginary fears. Here is undoubtedly a trying situation but he must rise to the occasion.

He should retain his mental equilibrium under all circumstances. Storms would blow around him but he should demonstrate the adequate strength and stability. He is not to get all lost rather try to ride over situation patiently. He should understand his responsibilities in front of emerging difficulties and work out the details of his future activities.

Once he gets hold of a blue print he may passionately involve himself in all the related activities. Time may come when he reaches the shores of success.

Rulers

There is another side of the picture. A common man lying low and all dispossessed, disappointed and frustrated generates extremely helpful situation fot the rulers. They can dominate over him without much of ruthlessness since he does not wish to assert. He lacks the courage to confront. That helps out the rulers to boast that they are peaceful and, in fact, their benevolent authority stands unchallenged. Minds of the ruler and the ruled appear to be tightly encased in this manner.

Helplessness of the Common Man

Well, there is a limit to which an individual can stretch his struggle. The repeated defeats rob him of his health, enervate his strength, crush his dynamism, ruin his courage and what not. He may be driven to a state of mind where he finds himself in the dungeon of darkness. If he fails and fails again, he may think of being knocked out from the battle of life. Time approaches when he thinks for surrender or submission or compromise.

The ideals of "try and try again" say of "permanent struggle" can be beautifully described in an article. Illustrious examples can be selected from the books of real or of imaginary history to prove that the desired results could be achieved by the people through untiring efforts. Those who have swung into action know the practical sides of the problems.

3

COMPULSIONS

"Good fortune will elevate even petty minds, and give them the appearance of a certain greatness and stateliness, as from their high place they look down upon the world, but in history noble and resolved spirit raises itself and becomes more conspicuous in the times of disaster and misfortunes."

Plutarch

For a common man, life is still a drudgery. He exists with the desire to live. There is no thrill, no excitement in his day to day living. What can he do ? He has no means to know it. He is obliged to accept things as they come to him. Since his know-how is limited, he therefore refuses to fight out his way. Even if he is persuaded to face the situation boldly the fear persists deeper in him that he would fail. That dampens his spirit. As a result, the old cycle of miseries continues. In the process, he gradually abandons his normal struggles also.

On the other hand, he if he does pursue his efforts half heartedly then spectacular results would not follow. At least, he can't depend upon chance factor to succeed. Miracles do not happen in the lives of those who are unfortunate and broken.

A great idea may at times be intuitively felt by some common man who is seized with some extraordinary situation in society. The state does not acknowledge him. They rather trains their guns against him so that he along with his idea is wiped out. History confirms as to how many such individuals had been liquidated. In the circumstances, how can common man hope to lead a meaningful life. Still it is his solemn duty to understand the conditions that are developing around. Times are fast changing. He can not afford to be an idle spectator. So he is to find out as to how he can help himself and be useful to the society of which he is a member. He is required to organise his thoughts and activities accordingly. He is the centre of the world. He is to act in totality and just integrating all what is going on in him and outside.

In the prophetic words of Acharya Rajneesh, "The world has known many saviours and the world is not saved. And the reason is that they were not alert. They started bragging their miracles, they started nursing their ego through their miracles. Then their miracles became only magic, just tricks, practised well. There was nothing like miracle in them. The greatest miracle in the world is that you should dance and disappear in the dance, then let the dance do whatever it can do—that should love and then disappear in the love ; then let the love do whatever it can do.

You cannot claim that you are doing it. You have already disappeared. In your disappearance is the whole possibility of some miracle happening.

So please do not guess, otherwise deep inside your love will remain half hearted, you are doing it for some purpose. And when love becomes a purpose, it is no longer love. Your joy would become phoney, because if you are joyful for something that happen in the world ; you are not really joyful, you are using joy, and if your dance is a means towards an end, it cannot be total.

Unless your dance is an end itself, there is no possibility of its being total. And only a total dance, an authentic love, a whole hearted joy perhaps may create some miracles around you. But you will not be the one who can brag about them. They will happen only when you are not.

God happens only when you have moved out of the way and left yourself totally empty, spacious. It is a strange phenomenon. Guest only comes when the host disappears."

Compulsions

A bright chap of humble origin may turn out to be an efficient and promising engineer or a doctor or an expert in some other profession, but his overall personality remains lopsided for a number of reasons. We are told that during his early life he was not suitably nurtured to match the future challenges that his career would have imposed. He is simply academically equipped and that is all.

Well, environment were not within his control. What could he do ? He has to transcend for competing with those who were born in more fortunate families. Still all his present difficulties should not dishearten him rather strengthen his faith in himself to do better.

He is not to play a second fiddle. He should daringly share more responsibilities, and compete with those who are trying to find fault with his up bringing. That would gradually augment his urges for self-reliance. It is a positive human trait, and would always drive his life in a right direction.

Adversities

Even if the circumstances are strained, the individual should not submit without trying his best. We do not advise him to break his head against the wall. He should also gain the experience of confronting defeats and failures gracefully. It is a great human quality and leads to maturity. That would help him to remain poised and composed even under hardships and to discover his best.

So individual may struggle and struggle valiantly. The result in the form of failure or victory should always appear to him of little significance. It has been noticed that those who have earned distinctions without much of serious efforts do not acquire sterling qualities through which human life is emblazoned.

The time may also come in the life of an individual when he fails to continue his struggle. Even the brave amongst the bravest cannot go beyond certain limits. It is only in such conditions we advise him to adjust with acceptable situations but even then his faith in the objectives to be actualised, should remain firm.

Course

Human civilisation is in the process of evolution. It has yet to reach such towering heights, that the higher possibie values for all times could be suggested by it. There would always remain a great need of human ennoblement. Special attention always required for the improvement of ethical side of the would be man. Such beliefs are to be cultivated, which may help a man to attain satisfaction in his inner side as well as in outside world. The first thing in this direction is to revive the spirit of service for the poor and the needy.

We speak of objectivity and rationality to our young men and women for appreciating the problems that our age is confronting. For instance, if I am comfortably situated in the environment, I can think of acquiring a detached view of things. On the other hand if I know that I am likely to be gunned down in next half an hour, or my daughter is likely to be raped somewhere, or my mother's life is threatened, I cannot remain poised or quiet or objective or rational in my thought and action. I would straightaway throw myself in the worlds of violence and illegality, whatever may be the consequences.

Reconstruction of human personality is not a scientific question exclusively. Man shall have to acquire certain high sounding characteristics. He has to fight against certain forces outside and many within himself. Life cannot be streamlined by scientific temper alone, it requires a strong support of the conscience.

World View

An average Indian is very much in the know of it that this "Samsara" is changing every moment. His time concept is cyclical. He evolves a range of traditions for regulating the normal scope of his life. He permits very little revision and ardently sticks to old positions since he fears that changes being proposed around have not been well thought out and these would only create instability and chaos and that would ultimatily make his life more miserable. On theoretical plane, he however understands, the factor of "change." He knows that he was once a child, grew up as a youth, and then as old man, but all this is a very slow process. That is why he insists that possibilities of gradual changes should be visualised and given a suitable direction. Their dynamics should be thoroughly grasped. The change "for the sake of change" is not a valuable idea. It should be motivated by its useful possibilities. So far future is concerned he knows that it would be different from the present but he does not apply his mind to peer into the womb of uncertainties. What we suggest is he should get out of his past habits, exercise his mind, think over the issues, plan out what can possibly be done, and then swing into action.

Quality in Life

Whatever may be the social position of an individual in the society, he should lend his weight for creating a better world. Life as it is, is a combination of joy and sorrow, of pleasure and pain, of success and failure and of shade and sunlight. It is dual in its character. An average Indian always places more emphasis on the fact that the real change would come within the individual by living gracefully. Dr. Karan Singh, a great scholar of Indian thought and civilisation, beautifully sums up, "I believe finally, that a divine destiny pervades the cosmos, a destiny not distant and remote but one in which in some mysterious way, each one is actively involved. I believe that the most effective means of fufilling that destiny is a combination of active outer involvement, in furthering human welfare and intense inner striving to reach the goal of spiritual realisation. I believe thus that the most eloquent prayer man has evolved is one that has resounded in India down through the corridors of time since the very dawn of civilisation. From the unreal lead me to real. From darkness lead me to the light. From death lead me to immortality."

Dr. Iqbal

We have been hearing the national song of Iqbal right from our school days, then over Radio and thereafter on TV again and again that "India is the best country of the world". Perhaps the great poet was trying to highlight the radiance of some classical greatness of his land. If an iota of common sense, a common man has, he raises his eyebrows on the claims of this great poet. He doubts over Iqbal's contention. It may be true as an ideal. We have to make India so by our efforts. We have not inherited it as such from our predecessors. Common man asks why he is always fed on poetry. Why is he advised time and again to make still more sacrifices ? He is told repeatedly to love his country but now he asks those who are at the helm of affairs whether they have such feelings for their mother land. Are they not required to set the examples for him ? At the moment, he is blank. He has no idealism, no destination, no cause to fight for.

Dictators and Czars

Still he holds on. Where does he seek his strength from ? He has of course some value system based on his understanding of religion. He falls back upon it in case of serious adversity. That provides him some psychic relief and strength. This is why he cannot help clinging to it. His overall conditions of living are growing harsher with the increasing complexities. The teeth of Modern State have become sharper. Economic constraints are multiplying. He looks at the oceans of wealth around. He cannot share even a drop of it. In the given conditions he has no choice but to submit. If he tries to wriggle out of stinking influences of all nonsense he would find himself more enchained.

Rulers of our times claim that they are very benevolent, reasonable and even humanists. They stand for non-violence. They permit bare minimum violence and that too under most unavoidable circumstances. They, first of all, take over the control of State and use its engines to grind their own axes and then other things follow. We are advised to read the records of their public speeches. These are made available for the contemporary public as well as for the future historians. Their real activities are performed behind the curtain. Even if it is conceded that they do not mean to decimate the common man since they assert of not being Czars and dictators and hold the positions through democratic means but the truth is that after being elected, their principal concern has been to remain in power. All other considerations are subservient to it. People do not aspire to become MPs and MLAs for rendering selfless services to their community. They are, in fact, prowling for distinguished chair simply for grabbing political power and through it lot of money.

Props

In the long and chequered history, common man had depended too much on real and imaginary props. He had long been blessed and guided by great incarnates, prophets, Yogis, Gurus and others. He followed their instructions as these were explained to him through their agents. All this has not saved him. The rulers had also been claiming to help him whereas the truth is that most of them had made the matters worst for him. His leaders had also failed him. Rather some of them were tyrants who had strangulated him. That is why his sufferings have all along been increasing in history. In the words of Faiz Anmed Faiz :

Chand roz aur, meri jan faqat chand hi roz.
Zulm ki chhoan men dam lene pe majboor hainham
Aur kuchh der sitam sah len tarap-len Ro-len
Apne ajdad ki miras hai, mazur Hain nam
Jism par qaid hai, jazbat pe zanjeeren hain
Fikr mahbus Hai, qufan pe taziren hain
Apni Himmat hai ke ham phir bhi jeye jate hain
Zindgi kya kisi muflis ki qaba hai jis-men
Har ghari dard ke paiwand lage jati hain
Lekin ab zulm ki mi-iad ke din thore hain
Ek Zara sabr, ke faryad ke din thore hain
Arsa-e dahr ki jhulsi hu-i virani mein
Hamko rahna Hai pe yun-hi to nahin rahna hai
Ajnabi hathon ka be-nam giranbar sitam
Aj sahna hai, hamesha to nahin sahna hai
Yeh tere husn se lipti hui alam ki gard
Anpni do roza jawani ki shikaston ka shumar
Chandni raton ka be-kar deahakta hua dard
Dil ki be sud tarap jism ki mayus pukar
chand roz aur, meri jan, faqat chand hi roz

(A few days more, my dear, only a few days. we are compelled to draw breath in the shadows of tyranny. For a while let us bear oppression, and quiver and weep. It is our ancestors legacy, we are blameless. On our body is the fetter, on our feelings are chains. Our thoughts are captive, or our speeches are censored ? It is our courage that even then we go on living. Is life some beggar's gown, on which every hour patches of pain are fixed? But now the days of the spur of tyranny are few. Patience one moment for the days of complaining are few. In the scorching desert of the space of this age, we must, part not stay like this. The nameless, the heavy oppression of foreign hands, today must be borne, nor always borne. The dusk of tribulations is enfolding your beauty and counting of the frustrations of our youth of twodays futile burning pain of moonlit nights, the heart's profitless throbbing, the body's despairing cry, a few days more, my dear only a few days).

Meaninglessness of Life

It is also argued by some eminent people that common man is an inconsequential creature since his awareness is limited. He has no means to collect data for arriving at correct decisions. He just breathes in "time and space" otherwise he is incapable of doing anything plausible. Even then it is not fair on their part to advise that he is a good-for-nothing fellow and carries no weight whatsoever. There is no dearth of such thinkers, writers and other qualified people who propose, discuss and enjoy discussing the meaninglessness of his life. They even extend their argument for life as a whole. He is not only Jean Paul Sartre. We have Sadhus, Yogis and others of so many schools of Indian philosophy who are found propagating, singing and making people believe that living on this earth is a purposeless activity. It is true there is injustice and tyranny all around, there is foul play but all that should not push us out of life. With all its heopelessness life is beautiful and worth living. We patronise and follow those schools of thought that strengthen man's will to struggle more vehemently so that he may wipe out all ugliness found in it. He will do it and win. Even if he dies in his efforts, he would leave his inspiring records. The following generation may pick up the threads once again.

There is another side of life. Common man gets no publicity of his performances even if these are at times laudable. There are some individuals who are engaged in some highly ennobling pursuits, but their work is not reported anywhere. They quietly move from one possibility to another all unseen and unnoticed. The press or radio or other means of communication do not come forward to appreciate their activities. So in all fairness, individual should try to get inward satisfaction over his output. He should feel happy as to how he has achieved his targets. That would develop his self esteem which is a positive trait and builds up a personality. On the other hand, if a boss speaks high of a worker, or press reports of a man doing a good job and he knows that his work is not admirable all out-side propaganda would not open the vistas of real happiness in him.

Marxist View

It is a popular Marxist view that if the economic conditions are hostile, the individual would miserably fail and the question of his discovering his own best is ruled out. When poverty is acute, the centre of life is focussed on hunger. Many eminent psychologists point out that the sex is also a conclusive instinct in shaping the destiny of a man. Every thing else is subservient to it. Some other great thinkers are of the view that lust for power is a very effective instinct. It goes a long way in shaping the futurity of man. Well, with increasing knowledge and growing life experiences many other factors have come to light which would help us in understanding man. With all regards for the findings of Marx, we cannot say that with him everything important was discovered and thereafter no development in man's further search is possible. Marx himself was not that dogmatic. It may be recalled that he refused to be dubbed as a Marxist in the evening of his life.

Opportunity

Much has been said against the deprivation under which people are destined to live, but we have come across a few people who could steal march over others who are better placed simply because they were denied opportunities.

The number of such people has, of course, been negligible, they are nevertheless there. We are to learn from their examples. Common man should bear in his mind that he is unaware of his real strength since most of his capacities are dormant. He has to discover them.

He is to understand that others should not decide so far as the vital issues of his own life are concerned. He has also to determine as to how he would think and act. He may visit temples, mosques, churches and other places of worship and pray for seeking help plus strength but he must try to depend also on his own self. He should not rest on deities and even the powerful men or leaders or institutions to shape his future. There is a saying that God would help him only if he helps himself. If this is the position of God, he can well appreciate what others would do for him.

There are many side issues of present life. His psychic conditions are very different from those of his predecessors. So long as he is on the winning side he talks tall of his efforts. In case of failures, he is nowhere. He has no hook, where he may hang his worries. He cannot apportion blame on some thing and feel relieved. He is therefore under stress, under strain. He is suffering from blood pressure, dyspepsia and many other fatal diseases of the kind.

All tyranny, violence and devastation had perpetuated in the past, but the common people could not be exterminated from the earth. They had continued to survive even under the long shadows of hunger, starvation and all forms of suppression. They were perhaps required to survive as underlings so that the rulers could dominate. So they had lived as historic necessity or say as a "necessary evil".

There have been slaves, shudras, serfs, landless peasants, unemployed and what not. Times have changed but they exist. We have to raise new patterns of thoughts which may help them to struggle with courage and conviction and take defeats with grace and dignity. All Men and Women are capable of reaching great heights. Law of life is to struggle and it does not suggest us to perish. We should always bear in mind that we are evolving. We do not stagnate. We cannot wait. In the words of Erwin Schrodingr, the noted German thinker of our times, "In everyday of our lives there occurs in us something of that evolution of our species which is still in full career. In fact every individual life, indeed every day in the life of the individual, has to represent, a part however small, of his evolution, a chisel stroke, however insignificant on the eternally unfinished statue of our species. For the whole of its tremendous evolution consists of myriads of such insignificant chisel strokes. And so at every step we have to change, overcome, destroy the form which we have had hitherto".

4

HUMAN CONDITIONING & SOCIAL LIFE

In the hour of death the only adequate consolation is that one has not evaded life, but has endured it. What a man shall accomplish, not accomplish does not lie in his power to decide; he is not the One who will guide the world ; he has only to obey. Every man has, therefore, first and foremost (instead of asking which place is most comfortable for him, which connection is most advantageous to him) to assure himself on the question of where Providence can use him if it so pleases Providence. The point consists precisely in loving his neighbour, or what is essentially the same thing, in living equally for every man. Every other point of view is contentions and however advantageous and comfortable and apparently significant his earthly rights, without attaching himself to just one single man, essentially existing equally for all men, he will, even though he apparently achieves nothing, even if he becomes exposed to the derision of the poor or to the ridicule of his superiors or to both insult and ridicule, yet in the hour of death, he will confidently, dare say to his soul, "I have done my best, whether I have accomplished anything, I do not know ; whether I have helped any one, I do not know, but that I have lived for them, that I do know, I know it from the fact that they insulted me. And this is my consolation, that I shall not have to take the secret with me to the grave, that I, in order to have good and undisturbed and comfortable days in life, have denied my kinship to other men, kinship with the poor, in order to live in aristocratic seclusion, or with the distinguished, in order to live in secret obscurity."

Kierkegaard

The Individual shall have to live in the present by associating himself with the society. He can, of course, reduce his contacts with it to some extent but these cannot be broken completely. Even Sadhus living in the caves of the Himalayas could not close up the same for all times. They also live at its fringes. The total "switch off" in this connection is impossible. Man is alwa ys in need of food, clothings, housing, fuel, light, electricity, medical aid, newspapers, schools and so on. Who is going to provide him all if he decides to move himself to self centre ? How long can he live at zero radius ? Moreover, what is the legitimacy of such a stand ? If he really wishes to live purposefully, he shall have to come out of himself and operate in the society more as a contributor and less as a receiver.

We have already emphasized that he is not a weakling. He should courageously and intelligently join hands with others and work out the essentials of his physical and other needs. If he exclusively depends upon his courage he may turn wreckless. If he takes shelter under the shade of his intelligence coupled with indifference he may not be able to decide anything. He would remain all hamletised. He should therefore first of all define the parametres of a good and happy life for himself. While doing so it must be ensured that he is not functioning against the interests of others.

Life & Death

We do not know about other animals but human beings know that they were once born and would die one day, since they see people passing through this life routine every moment. Still, as individuals they try to live with the conviction that they would never die. They wish to overcome their fear of death, but the death persists. Its fear cannot therefore be banished from their thinking.

"The Cradle", Nobokov, the eminent American novelist,said "rocks above the abyss and the common sense tells us that an existence is but a brief crack of light between two eternities of darkness. Although, the two are identical twins, man as a rule, views his pre-natal abyss with more calm than the one he is heading for". Right from his birth he gets conditions around.

He grows under their influences. As an infant he is all a liability. He is not in a position to have his own way. Free development for the impulses that nature has planted in him is not permitted. He also comes in conflict with the interests of others.

Urban Life

Life in the big cities is changing very fast. The simple ideal of decent and good living that was evolved over centuries is no longer in vogue. People are drifting to short cuts i.e. corruption, loot, thefts and so many other vicious activities. In recent times their material needs have shot up but capacities to meet them have not comparatively increased. As a result, so many dishonest means of raising money have been discovered by them. That is obviously not in the overall interests of a society which is largely based in rural side. We see its ugly demonstration, vulgarity in so many forms spreading and moral bankruptcy written large on the faces of modern citizens.

New Data

A new workable programme is to be drawn up, propagated and put into operation. So many crimes are being committed in the cities. All do not come into the lime light. Whatever is published and noticed confirms that chaos is increasing all round. There is hardly any side of life which does not appear to be mutilated. We have to make frantic efforts in searching examples of decent and manly living in our cities and publicise the same. That would help people in learning what and how they should think, do, and achieve. Press is doing a great disservice in this regard. We are given to read all that is bad. The masses are anxiously looking for new props and nothing meaningful is being done in this direction. We are to know about social, economic and political scene through newspapers, Radio, TV etc. Whatever is noticed through these means is pathetic. We should try to understand the complexities of modern life. Its degeneration is accepted even by the so-called hopeful and optimists. Politics moves fast and attracts people, but that is not so in the domain of social problems. During these years, we have had no movement of social reforms at national level. So this side of our life has been stagnating for long. Many corrupting influencies have creeped therein. For instance, we have had an old social disease of "dowry system". It has now become fatal. We notice its disastrous influences in our families. There is no check against it in the real sense of the term. We see people competing with one another in giving away dowries to their daughters. In the process they ruin themselves and inspire others to imitate their example.

Social Work

We have more of social scientists, sociologists, social workers and so on, but we do not find dedicated social reformers and crusaders on the Indian firmament. People are fairly religious even today but religion has been commercialised. It is no longer being used as a force to reform the society. We honour Swamis like Dayananda Saraswati and Vivekananda and many others, but they have no successors and even sincere followers. Conditions are therefore drifting from bad to worse. It is high time for some people to rise to the occasion.

In recent years a lot of data regarding our social life has been collected. It is discussed, interpreted and elaborated by highly qualified and competent professional groups. They throw up many valuable conclusions. This is all a brilliant academic effort. Hereafter their task is over. Their findings are to be converted into workable programmes for spreading out new social awareness. The issues to be grappled with are much bigger than preparation of well documented reports by the specialists. We have to launch therefore big social movements of the epochal order. Only then fresh psychic conditions would emerge and new attitudes be formed.

Real Task

Times are fast changing. We hope that international peace would prevail. Wars would be banished in the future history, and important constructive activities would be intensified on war footing. Their principal objective would be to stimulate the people to understand their responsibilities and be ready to meet even the most trying situations. They are first of all concerned with their social and economic emancipation. They have suffered too much in their long and chequered history.

They are to be provided with new thoughts for effectively tackling their present social and economic and other problems.

Their is no dearth of information. What we lack, at the moment, is, the will to act with force and work for our transformation. New thought systems should help people to look up socially, economically, politically, mentally and even morally. They should stand fast against traditional vices of casteism, communalism, regionalism, fatalism, escapism, and timidity. We should not permit our hearts to be swayed against our heads. We must know what is a balanced mind and understand the position of others and then act. A serious effort is to be made first by raising our own beings and then of helping others. Such values are to be rooted in the deeper depths of the psyche of a common man. Position, at the moment, is that many centuries old traditions are well entrenched as if these were elements of spiritual greatness. That occupy attention areas of a common man. We have to inspire him for their re-examination and that is possible if he acquires scientific temper to a certain degree. There is nothing wrong if he studies those details of his personality which make him what he is. With this he would achieve some psychic stability and then he would not be easily provoked. His reactions would be thoughtful. He would participate in the scheme of things carefully and decisively. He would not be easily led away by false and baseless propaganda. Now he is a wrestler in the arena not just a spectator watching the performance of others.

Human Mind

Human mind is formless yet it is such a phenomenon that had engaged the attention of so many prophets, saints, thinkers, philosophers, psychologists, writers and even of the common people through all times. It is still being explored. Its length is enormous, its breadth very large, its depths cannot be fathomed and heights have no limits. We do not know the end points of its frontiers. Though it is not infinite, it is very close to it.

It has many functions to perform. It observes, reads, studies, remembers, thinks, speaks, examines, inquires, doubts, rejects, accepts, criticises, evaluates, appreciates and even denounces. All thls does not exhaust the list of its functions.

It, receives data in the form of words, and it is not a photographic camera. Whatever it possesses it is in some 'form' not 'in content.'

Its possibilities of integration and disintegration of ideas are enormous. It is capable of making combinations and permutations of all kinds and that too very quickly. It has gigantic power of calculations. In addition to this, it is just like an ocean containing habits, traditions, memories, prejudices, beliefs and what not. Developments of modern science and technology are influencing its behaviour in so many ways. We read a lot regarding brain washing techniques that are being practised in many modern societies. We know individuals get addicted to many narcotics for seeking some artificial peace of mind since it is a very sensitive part of human body. It is one of the principal responsibilities of an individual to ensure that his mental capacities are always expanding, improving and perfecting. In other words he is continuously enriching his mind. It is the fountain of all creative powers. His potentialities of solving even the intricate problems intuitively are also acknowledged. Man is capable of discovering and inventing of something that is unknown till date. He moves on and on through observation, investigation and imagination. The period of incubation of ideas in the human mind may vary from individual to individual but it goes without saying that mind goes forth. It is neither Eastern nor Western. It is human. If we try to compartmentalise it, we shall reduce its capacities. In fact, much of it is formed before the individual is capable to understand as to what has happened to it. Its growth is a quiet process of long duration.

Transformation

Its transformation in the light of new knowledge and modern requirements is a delicate task since it is more often arrested by the chains of habits and attitudes. With all its possibilities individual needs help from outside. He is to be educated, persuaded, guided and even indoctrinated ; this formation cannot be left to chance. Each mind acquires a method of learning, knowing and understanding of thing due. Gradually, it is shaped and chiselled. It is then capable of making independent decisions with the abilities and capacities so acquired. The past is always at work in the formulation of a man's mind. It may at times drive him to depend upon those judgements which are no longer relevant. It is therefore imperative that he should keep his mind ready to make judicious judgements and unlearn those things that are detrimental and are still being practised.

Acharya Rajneesh sums it up beautifully, "Our whole training of mind is such that we are made afraid of insecurity and our whole life we are trying for safety – financially, politically, religiously, in every dimension we want to be secure. But security means death, a living death. It means tomorrow will be simply a repetition of today, and today is a repetition of yesterday. Are you living ? Is there is a dance in your life ? Are you moving growing, risking, taking the challenges of dangerous path ? In the acceptance of the danger, in the acceptance that anything can happen any moment life comes to its best, to its fullest"

Open Mind

An open mind is free from general constraints and imaginary fears. It is in a position to call spade a spade. Well, it is not a vacant mind. It is just like a newly constructed instrument and that functions more effectively.

The prophets and leaders of different great religions and lofty ideologies endeavour that the human mind should somehow be tied to certain great purpose or to some high sounding principles. It is also believed that such efforts are extremely useful for the individuals. Then they do not run from pillar to post and get a set direction in achieving their objectives. So valuable guidance is made available to them as to how they should march on the paths of life. They are given to feel that their thoughts are now based on the unshakable rocks of sound beliefs and their minds are thus fortified with certainties. Are they open minds even then ? Yes, only in the early stages.

Closed Minds

This process works for some time, and life moves on. The ideas that were once cultivated with lot of enthusiasm becomes stale with the passage of time but the minds of the people are still stuffed with them. They do not even think of reconsidering them. They would do and die for their beliefs. Their consciousness is not pricked even when they act wrongly under the dictates of their beliefs. Then they begin to decay since the closed minds do not get the opportunity of further growth. Like body, human mind should also take exercise to retain its vitality, creativity and originality.

Mental Disorders

We find that the psychological disorders are increasing all over the world. The human mind, in fact, is not rising to the occasion since it is unable to meet the challenges of expanding and deepening complexities of our times. If we do not try to improve upon its thinking capacities, there is a limit beyond which it would not be able to stretch and then collapse under the weight of deadly situations is inevitable.

The common man should learn how to face unusual situations that come in life. He should not get disturbed or excited under the weight of increasing tensions. Whatever may be the intensity of the threats that try to crush him, he should retain his balance or patience or poise. Storms would come and go. He should remain firm and wait for the suitable moments to arrive. Time and tide do not wait. The activities of the mind are inside but its tangible influences are noted outside. These are two sides of a bow.

5

SCIENTIFIC TEMPER

"The new man contains my whole philosophy about life and how it should be lived—in totality, intensity, in wholeness, so that we are not just dragging ourselves from the cradle to the grave, but we can make each moment a tremendous rejoicing, a song, a dance, a celebration......

Nuclear weapons and all destructive measures are a preparation for a global suicide. The old man has decided to die. It is up to the intelligent people in the world to disconnect with the old man before he destroys you too......It is a great responsibility for the new generation, for the young people to renounce the past.

In the past, religions used to renounce the world. I teach you to love the world so that it can be saved and to renounce the past totally and irrevocably. Be discontinuous."

Acharya Rajneesh

Science is neither national, nor religious, nor regional and nor communal. Its seeds are lying in human necessities. It grows as a result of persistent efforts by human mind through observation, searching, researching, verifying, investigating, analysing, calculating and above all thinking dispassionately. In ordinary sense of the term, it helps in increasing our powers both of construction and destruction. It is, therefore, something amoral. The moral element to it is to be provided by the user of the science so that it may usefully serve the mankind.

Learning

It is unfair to decide that the science should be taught in the schools only. Most of our people do not prosecute their studies, but it is very important that they should understand the broad principles and applications of science in their day-to-day life. They should rather acquire scientific temper for handling their problems. All means of communication, namely radio, television, press etc. should be directed to achieve this end. Scientific orientation would help the people to acquire a right perspective for discharging their normal functions.

Specialisation

There is another side of the problem. We have already ushered into the age of specialisation. The highly qualified scientists and technologists are there who may be able to render very useful services in this period of civilisational crisis. They know a lot about something small, smaller and the smallest. In fact, their bits of knowledge are to be integrated for building up a mighty edifice of new human knowhow. The explosion of knowledge in our times is a fact that cannot be brushed aside. We dicuss it. We learn about it, but full advantages from it are not flowing to the people. Some thing is to be done in this connection. We should not leave all this to chance. Efforts are required to ensure that uses of sciences and technologies sould expand. The structure of education should by modified and strengthened for increasing our awareness in this respect.

Present dilemma

Over the years each branch of science has been developing its own terminology. That is understood only by those who are concerned with it exclusively. This makes specialist of one field a layman in all other branches of knowledge. Where does a common man stand in a situation like this ? His over all level of education is very low. So the question of his understanding ins and outs of new discoveries is not possible since these are highly complicated. He has no means whatsoever to appreciate and understand as to how the big strides in knowledge are being made in different fields of science. He hears of them just as he listens to his prayers in Sanskrit quietly which are beyond his comprehension. Time has come that important and useful parts of specialised knowledge should be "made easy" to the extent possible so that common man should be able to grasp its essence and then apply it for his own advancement. If suitable steps are not taken well in time, it is feared that progress of science and technology would get further away from the larger sections of our society.

Scientific Temperament

We must give credit to the scientists for throwing up all useful data by their persistent efforts and at the same time for their being unassuming and humble in their normal conduct. They do not claim themselves to be the custodians of all truths. They are not the champions of certainty. They submit that they might be found wrong. Their minds are open. They would accept new findings collected on the basis of more reliable data and abandon their past positions with no regret. They take pride in not being infallible. That is why scientific knowledge is always in the process of remaking.

Once scientific temper is spread amongst the people to a reasonable degree, it would then be easily possible to inspire them for remodelling their patterns of lives. That is why it is asked as to how we should generate scientific temper the millions and millions who are generally not educated. They may be advised to examine their day-to-day performance critically. They should verify, and compare the data of their outputs with those of others. They should visualise as to how things could be further improved. They may approach to those who know better or have achieved success in their performance. They may be advised to examine their thoughts. Even beliefs may be scrutinised. The traditions should be looked into. In short the very foundations of their lives beyond Biology may be investigated.

The approach on these lines would liberate their minds from all kinds of preconceived ideas. It would gradually help them to look at their prevailing conditions objectively and dispassionately. In the process their minds would turn all transparent. The element of past prejudices would then find no place. It would significantly touch the material side of the people. The farmers would be ready to accept the scientific means of growing better harvests. The workers would know better regarding the use of machines in the factories. Our women would know how to rear their children better. Our students would look more for technical and professional training.

Humanities

By emphasising scientific education we do not mean to underestimate the importance of teaching art, literature, philosophy, history and other social sciences in our school and colleges. A right balance is to be struck. Simultaneous growth on all possible sides relating to human life is absolutely necessary.

Of late, there has been a serious upheaval in the domain of scientific thought. Science and technology had based their principles and activities on the nineteenth century ideas of matter. Now the very base stands rejected in the light of new findings. Our scientists used to pooh-pooh the ideas of spirit and spirituality. In our times new scientific thinking has left matter and materiality behind. Indian scientists feel elated on discovering that modern science is getting closer to philosophy. Many of them believe it a home coming i.e. back to the mother of all knowledge, philosophy.

Past Values Through Back Door

People living in the cities and towns go to the fields, factories, industries, offices and other places for earning their livelihood, but they have to carry their total personalities with them including their beliefs as well as many other traits. If their minds are backward looking, narrow, parochial, sick, insecure and thoughts negative and diseased, they wculd fail to integrate themselves with others on broader humanistic principles. They would prefer to remain in their past holes. Even in the new environment they look for the people of their own class or caste or region or religion and make all efforts to befriend them. They would not therefore come out of the caves of their past darkness rather feel safe and secure under the influence of existing conditions.

Matter does not end here. They fail to outgrow on account of their narrow loyalties and live with blurred visions of history. That would ultimately affect their efficiency too. At the same time their attitudes leave far-reaching repurcussions on those whole organisations where they are working. Gradually their tendencies travel in the whole systems and as a result, their over all functioning is adversely affected. That gives rise to groupism and rivalries of so many kinds which damage the production too. Positive spirit of competition is not permitted to grow and short cuts are found for manipulating incomes. They do not improve their efficiency and remain in the jackets of their past attitudes. If detailed investigations are conducted by some neutral agencies it would be found how our Industrialisation is being choked by these shortcomings.

We should therefore institute such training programmes at a very large scale and inspire our people to think in broader terms. The irony is that they do not know what they are doing since all their activities are spontaneous. They do not understand their failings. They have to unlearn certain things and go to their work with open minds.

Present Situation

The new humanistic values that are growing popular all over the world are closer to the scientific thought, but a common man in India is not in a position to understand and absorb them at the moment. An occasional speech of a great leader may suggest the necessity of such a temper but that cannot cultivate it. For augmenting individual produce in the fields of agriculture and industry, he may use scientific and technological means but that does not automatically bring him closer to secular and scientific thinking. His psyche remains under the spell of the past traditions and beliefs. It is not transformed. For him the application of science and technology is for certain limited objectives, whereas the deeper side of his life, remains reserved for realising something else.

New Education

We should advocate rigorous but simultaneous ideological and technological education in our schools, colleges and universities. The pioneers of our New Education Policy should meet the challenge of national transformation with courage. The ideological foundations should be raised on the teachings of Nanak, Chishti, Raja Ram Mohan Roy, C.F. Andrews, Tagore, Gandhiji, Nehru, Azad, JP, M.N. Roy, Bhave, and others. There is no harm in learning from the outside sources i.e. from the West, but ideas so borrowed should fit within the framework of our ethos. We do not mean to indoctrinate people for acquiring aggressive Nationalistic feelings despising others. We only wish that they should build up their own will and reconstruct their lives in the given Indian conditions. New and important values to be spread and impressed upon the people are namely self-reliance, self-help, open minds, cooperating with others, thriftiness, but decent living, clean and honest public life, striving to acquire scientific temper etc.

All this would ultimately generate new consciousness and a new spirit of commitment. We always need the rehearsal of the messages of peace, since without it no progress is possible. At the same time emotional arousal of the people is absolutely necessary for building up new dams, canals, schools, colleges, hospitals, development of waste lands, roads, huge industries etc. They must feel convinced that these steps are for their own advancement. Those who matter should not forget that nation building activities are qualitatively different from organising electioneering campaigns. These may at times meet severe opposition from the established culture and that is to be met valiantly.

Wars

Man is a peculiar animal. He is at once a supporter of change and stability. He engineers reforms, revolts, rebellions and even revolutions for change. On the other hand, he works out number of beliefs, ideals, laws, organisations, constitutions and so on, so that order and stability in the society are not jeopardised. So these are two banks through which the river of his life is to flow. All the times river is turning this way or that. It does not move straight. In our times, the science and technology have equipped man with certain unusual powers to make or mar present and future. On the one hand, he has piled up most deadly weapons in his arsenal. Does he mean to use them for killing sparrows and other animals ? No. This is obviously for those men and women who do not see eye to eye with him. Others are also not sitting idle. They also scare him. So this is the situation. First of all he should shed his own fears. Others would follow suit. He must lead in this respect. This is the first ideal to to be followed. Alternative to peace is total destruction. There is no third choice.

Text Books

We may pick up any text book of a primary school. We find so many ideals stated there in a few lessons. The children are advised to know them, but unfortunately the pressures of real life would be so heavy that everything learnt in that tender age goes awry.

Life

We receive life as it comes to us. We make all efforts to improve our standard of living in material sense of the term but we prefer to live from hand to mouth in respect of our value system. If justice and fair play demand from us to lose something, we refuse and put up vain arguments in our defence. Selfishness is well entrenched both in our heads and hearts. We try to justify our wrong actions. We cook up reasons as if our efforts are related to basic instinct may be of self-preservation. The truth is other way round. It is one thing to press for two square meals or ask for opportunities of moderate living, but it is something quite different to have everything for oneself and leave nothing for others.

Role

If the society is coercive and the individual feels insecure or say feels suffocated, how far would he tolerate ? There is a limit. He may either submit and lose all interest in life or rebel against the order being imposed. If he opts for submission, he is helping the society to decay as he is advocating not to struggle when he should. If he chooses to rebel, he is inviting all kinds of hazards for himself as well as for his family but in the process he is remaking the future.

He should select the path that helps him to look forward and drives the society to reconstruct itself. Higher ideals help in inspiring the people for taking up the cudgels against those forces that do not permit him along with others to improve their lot. Once correct and achievable ideals are well understood, adapted and then practised, individuals begin to ascend. They do not remain men of straw that they used to be, i.e. prior to professing of those ideals.

6

NEW QUEST

"We need a philosophy, a direction, and a hope if the present state of indecision is not to lead us to chaos. The agitation of minds, all eager for new light, suggests that we may be on the boundaries of new life. We are in search of a religious message that is distinctive, universally valid, sufficient and authoritative, one that has an understanding of the fresh sense of truth and the awakened social passion which are the prominent characteristics of the religious situations today. Belief may be difficult but the need for believing is inescapable. We may present struggling and inspiring humanity with a rational faith, which does not wreck the free spirit of man by arbitrary dogmas or hesitating negations, a new vision of God in whose name we can launch a crusade against the strange cults which are now competing for mastery over the souls of men".

Dr. S. Radhakrishnan

Common man would set aside his traditional anchors of security namely caste, creed, religious fanaticism etc. if he is fully convinced that their influences really drive him to backwardness. He should examine their utility in view of his present conditions. He is no longer living in his centuries old village all cut off from the world. Times have changed. His dependence on traditional ways of life is reducing. Well before throwing them away he may dispassionately consider if these are really helpful to him especially when he is involved in creating a new social order. He is to ensure that he is really creating a more helpful and better world. He should not out for an age in which our children should carry daggers, swords, guns, stenguns and other sophisticated weapons on their shoulders for wiping out their opponents. They would be in need of those implements, sophisticated implements that may help them to increase production in agriculture and in industry and earn higher incomes.

Village zamindars, the corrupt police officers and the other agents of exploitation and suppression are to be removed from the scene. Selfish priests are to be liquidated. New means of better living are to be created. New ideals of brotherhood, love and equitable distribution of the production are to be realised. All this may lead to a bit of chaos for a short while in the initial stages but we must act firmly. Gradually dust settles and new social equilibrium would emerge. That would be the real beginning of India's entry in the modern age. A new environment would be noticed as a result of forward looking and progressive attitudes. There would be no suffocation rather desires to expand would pulsate amongst the people. Far reaching changes would gradually set in. New ideologies would join hands with expanding technology. Streams of fresh thought and new science would commingle for becoming a future river of our onward march. Indian scientists and technologists are seriously at work. Their number would be increasing still further, but we are failing on the front of ideology at the moment.

Updating of Ideals

Ideals are not divinely ordained but are generally thrown up by those who are talented and seized with the destiny of the people. While updating the same many old ones are to be set aside, some are to be modified, a few new ones are to be tried and experimented. Longevity of a particular ideal should not be the reason for its perpetuation. It is to be evaluated in view of our changing social, economic political and other conditions.

A common man with average or say with minimum level of education and knowledge is not intellectually equipped to appraise the utility of a particular ideal critically. Still he receives bits of information from so many sources. These may be correct or even otherwise but get deposited in his thought apparatus. His mental framework is already formed to a certain degree. The new information is processed therein. He draws his own conclusions. If some thing new is not fitting well in the system already built up by him, he would denounce it. Serious application of mind for determining the usefulness of an idea not done. He adopts an easy course and submits to knowledge plus wisdom he has already acquired. That is dear to him. In the circumstances improvement in his personality would be bare minimum.

The weight of the past is very heavy on the minds of own rural folk. It does not permit many well meaning ideas to work on them and that could have transformed their lives in general. Records are there to testify as to how frequently the just and fair causes were crushed and these could not make headway for want of support.

New Approach

It is absolutely necessary on the part of those who wish to work amongst the people that they remain down to the earth. No high flown and empty ideas. The need of our times is careful planning and infallible will to work. Only then they would be able to see deeper in the lives of the people. Individual can perhaps catch hold of a few ideals and may try to actualise their content. But in case of society the task is not that simple. People would not easily commit to something which does not appeal to them straight. Say advice to work more falls on deaf ears. They would easily find fault in the proposed scheme of things. Here lot of organisational ability is called for from those who wish to move the society. Well, if they succeed in doing so even to a small extent, it is a great achievement.

In the past, it used to be only a microscopic minority that grappled with the crises. There were few amongst the very few who really picked up the cudgels and went straight into the heart of things. Now times are changed. The few would not be able to achieve much since the problems have become very difficult and intricate. Now men in fairly large number are to be drawn into the struggles for realising objectives. Issues have become multi dimensional. Tried methods are no longer of serious importance. New paths are to be laid. We have to persuade those millions of millions who are not ready to accept changes in their thinking. Mind it, they are not fools and knaves. They may be at times well meaning, sincere and dedicated men and women too.

In our circumstances, it is absolutely necessary that proposed approach should be related to the real needs of the people at large. We should lay emphasis only on those points that may help them to grow and expand. Our idealism must be compatible with the reality of their conditions. Once minds are set, thoughts turn straight and actions are taken accordingly, in due course benefits would flow to then. Well a lot of patience is required from those who are swinging into action. Passionate participation of the people in the struggle for realising the principal objectives of life is very important. They would respond enthusiastically if they are convinced that those who have come to work amongst them are true to the salt.

Indifferent People

There are people who maintains stoic indifference to all kinds of struggles and movements. They adhere to their personal problems and in the process show disregard to the important issues concerning life and society. Well, they may claim that they are not engaged in any destructive activity, but the fact remains they have very limited constructive role to play.

Still they are protagonists of peace and order. They believe there should be no upheavals, no stir, no agitations and so on. They would always insist that the trouble shooters should be severely dealt with and if possible they may even be wiped out. Such elements are fairly large in our society. If they have some expressed ambition they would not mind if others are also working like them.

Our resolving for peace does not mean as if there would be no agitations, no strikes and so on in the months or years to come. So long as an individual is meeting injustice of some sort, he would certainly try for the change in his conditions. This of course, goes without saying that he may so conduct his affairs that more help flows from his work to others than he expects from them. Transcending the ideal of enlightened self-interest from the selfish style of living where his instincts obviously drive him is also a big task. Here lies the reconstruction of man from inside out a great step forward.

Ideology

If we talk of man and think of men, we are Gandhians. If we talk of men and think of men, we are Socialists or Communists of some brand. If we talk of man and think of man we are Vedantins. If we talk of men and think of man, we are liberals. These are broad principles of those ideologies that are prevalent. Let us locate our ideological position. Wherever we are situated, there is need of love, service, sacrifice, fair play decency and so on. Life is still begging for all these qualities from men and women in general. We have noticed the hollowness of the Gandhians, violence of the Communists, indifference of the Vedantins and tyrannies of the liberal democrats.

Gandhians do not uphold the essentials of Gandhism. Communists are fighting with ex-communists. Vedantins have a long history of disputes and dissensions amongst themselves. They have no meeting points. The so-called democrats and capitalists had fought the most devastating wars of modern history.

We think of man and men, as one thing. These are two sides of one coin. Individual is not subservient to his society rather its builder and creator. We look forward that workable system of society which should admit the possibilities of even major and profound changes in its operations without the use of violent means.

Truth

We must set our minds on certain objectives and strive to realise them. Instead of muddling through, we should be clear about our means and ends as far as possible. The suppression of a common man is a reality and it cannot be dismissed as a sheer propaganda. The powerful in the society are at once cunning and clever. They work out plausible reasons in their defence for justifying their high handedness. Through sophisticated arguments the character of suppression is not changed though same is hidden.

Logical Conclusions

There is explosion of knowledge all around. The conditions are transforming so fast that we cannot have a pause and sit down for the refinement of our ideas so that a good part of new knowledge is learnt and then digested. Our wisdom stagnates and knowledge is not being grasped. We are soon being taken over by new conditions and cannot help wresting with them. In the given situation, we cannot afford to wait and see and draw thoughtful and logical conclusions with cool and peaceful minds. Every thing appears to be under huge stress. Pressure of day-to-day problems is mounting.

New Approach

Many intelligent people have abandoned the world of high idealism. So there is vacuum. Some of the people are satisfied with the idea of collecting or hoarding money. For men there is no other ambition more important than this. It assures them comfortable living to a great degree. There are others in the society who try to seize political power and then go for its use, misuse and abuse. Fair means to climb up in life are always long, thorny and tortuous. Who has time and patience to adopt them ? Short cuts to grab some forms of power are being searched.

Idle Thinkers

There had been no dearth of lazy and indifferent intellectuals in our society. They are all the time discussing issues from so many angles but with no will to grapple. They wish others should come forward, meet perils and change the rotten conditions. They should be left to themselves for grumbling as to how and why people are failing. Unfortunately we have a tradition of respecting even such people even though they are good for nothing.

Individual's Role

Life is an on going phenomenon. It does not stop and is changing. What can common man do ? Well, he is not a slave, that is true, but he is not that omnipotent who may command the situation. He has to assert and adjust simultaneously. There is no other alternative. He has to set up bridges with the society for his very survival and onward progress. Being too small, he cannot carry the world with him but should demonstrate enough of vitality so that he is not swept away by those forces that are working against him. He is supposed to extend his support to those who mean to help him materially and otherwise. He may not be living by bread alone but it is his principal need. As soon as it is moderately met, he must strike for new horizons.

Cooperative Efforts

With expanding industrialisation and increasing agricultural outputs, production of material goods for human use has gone up enormously. With that, the desire for more production has not been satisfied, rather clamour for producing still more has been intensified. Man's ambitions are always higher than his possibilities. We set our targets and strive to achieve them as per the schedule already laid out by us. For this large scale cooperative efforts are expected from the individual, society and State. Suitable institutions are to be founded so that their work could be well coordinated. Raising of an epochal movement in this connection is, therefore, very important. We can think and plan of equitable distribution only when we have huge stocks of our necessities available otherwise we shall have to distribute denials and frustrations. Who would like to share them ? So it is the solemn duty of all concerned to lend their support for building up healthy and efficient cooperatives. People would either cooperate or perish. They are left with no other choice since all other alternatives that are known to mankind are harsher.

State

Common man should, therefore, honour his commitments to society and its power which is vested in the state. It is generally condemned as an "engine of oppression" by those who are exploited by its activities. The irony is that the beneficiaries do not speak high of it since they always strive for more and more advantages from it. As state is omnipotent in a society, its scare is felt and experienced by all.

We cannot wriggle out of it, and still insist that common man should preserve his identity under all political systems. At times his conditions are so strained that he is compelled to rebel. He is to safeguard his freedoms. There is a powerful compass fitted somewhere in his mind which should provide him the details as to how he is supposed to proceed under the given conditions. He should exercise his own judgements in his day to day life. It does not mean that while doing so, he need not share his view with others. He should try to ascertain the correctness of his views. If considered necessary, he may take corrective actions. Times are dawning when leaders alone would not make all important decision. All philosophies, ideologies, religions, reformers, leaders, friends and others are there. He may try to know as to what they would have advised under the conditions, but ultimately all decisions relating to his own life should be made by him. In the process he may commit mistakes but that would finally help him to acquire experience and maturity. These are great human assets which are not easily achievable.

State and Individual

Much can be said for and against this phenomenon, but we cannot reverse the march of history. Individual shall have to adjust and the state should try to accommodate him at his terms, if possible. Here the tactlessness af the individual may cost him heavily. He can help and advise the State to discharge its functions correctly. So long as it is responding to the legitimate demands of the poor and downtrodden, its decisions should be honoured and respected.

With the passage of time, the accelerated industrialisation would lead to rew stages of developments in our parts of the world. Individual's dependence on machines would increase. He may ask for more of material comforts, relief from hard work and even additional leisure. It is difficult to anticipate all the challenges of those times. Well, people are to be kept in ferment on long term basis so that they do not shirk work. Human progress ultimately rests on hard work even when prosperity increases. Living luxuriously does not mean living well or even doing well. We hope suitable ways and means would be discovered which may help the individuals to work more and locate the best of their latent possibilities. The thrill of life does not lie in living in ease and comfortably rather in struggling and ascending to achieve something better and higher. Human mind shall have to continue its intellectual and other exercises for acquiring higher levels of creativity and inventiveness, otherwise it would become lazy and indifferent. It is not meant for discharging routinised items of work. Its sensitivities should not get dimmed. Individual should not run away from the problems posing threats. He matters. Once he loses his grip over the conditions he would exist in time and space but only as a non-descript.

Groups

At present, distinct professional groups namely army personnel bureaucracy, farmers, traders, industrialists, working class in the public and privat industries, teachers etc. enjoy the support and protection of the State more than the left outs in the society. There may be variations in the quantum of the support these groups receive, but it is nevertheless there. The interests of such groups are not simply being protected rather promoted in accordance with the pressure they can exert. Here performance is seldom a criterion. Merit is not important. Pressure for creating dislocation works as a real threat to those who rule. All workers are not embodiments of virtues and an exploited group of people. All capitalists are not plunderers. All rulers are not exploiters. All States are not cruel suppressors. Well, many workers are receiving more than their due at many places. Many capitalists have been ruined over these years. Many rulers have worked for the suppressed. Many states are doing quite well. We have observed another phenomenon in our times that many of our people are at once exploited and exploiters. This is an exciting topic for further studies. If it is thoroughly examined, many sensational details of human life of our times would come to lime light.

Disorganised Mankind

People at the grass roots level have also instinct to survive which forces them to look up for some defence mechanism so that they could somehow exist. Once it is ensured to a certain degree, their desire for self expression becomes very important. The poor of the world may get sensitized with it any moment.

Most of the states have done very little so far to ameliorate peoples' lot. This information is spreading rapidly in many parts of the world. Where are those leaders of society who are supposed to come forward and take up their grievances ? The present effort of those who are at the helm of affairs is just like pouring a glass of water in the ocean. This is why the fate of the millions and millions who are disorganised and happen to live in the farflung areas of the country is misearable. Who would reach them ? These poor people may not be knowing what to do. They just adhere to traditional ways of their lives or say to certain taboos. That provide them some ray of hope which atleast help them to survive as destitutes. Their consciousness straightway responds to fatalism, escapism and other negative philosophies. So they do not look up and roam about in the blind alleys of their past thoughts.

They are to be attended to. That is the principal task confronting our age. We should keep them in view while redefining the roles of man, society and state. That is the real task. We are in need of such movements which may help in the brain storming of the people at the bottom level. That would lead to restructuring many of our present institutions.

We are very fond of blaming others for all our failures and failings. Time has come for severe self-analysis and of proposing of fresh suitable values.

World of Common Man

The common man has very few choices. He is never out of the world and latter is also never out of him. He is its badly integrated part i.e. some thing not very important. How can he move the wheels of history ? First of all he is to realise it in himself that he matters. He has to prepare himself to do some thing by which society is helped. He should lend a helping hand to its developmental activities. He has to bear in mind that he is to prove himself to be its asset.

If he wishes that others should not exploit him, it is his solemn duty to prove beyond doubt he does not mean to exploit others. He has one mouth to eat but two eyes to see, two ears to hear, two arms to work, two legs to walk and a multi purpose body. He can certainly do much more than to meet the needs of one mouth. Since he has the support of so many physical organs. Above all he has a versatile and fertile brain which has many manipulative powers.

Schophenhauer says, "Man is at bottom a wily and terrible animal. We know him only as what we call civilisation has tamed and trained him : hence we were alarmed by the occasional breaking out of his true nature. But whenever locks and chains of law and order are cast off and anarchy comes in, he shows himself what he really is". Well, these are the views of a great philosopher but certainly not of an eminent builder. His remarks should not stop us from contemplating to plan correct development of human being. We are committed to help him in rearranging his world in peaceful order. We have to fight against such tendencies as negate his positive, constructive and useful powers.

7

CENTRE OF HUMAN LIFE IS SOCIETY

"In every inquiry about duty we must keep in mind the natural superiority of men over cattle and other animals. Animals deal only in sensual pleasures and are by instinct impelled to seek it. But the mind of man is nurtured by study and contemplation. He is always investigating or doing something".

Cicero

"...... The reason why Europe is going to dogs is a course that it has accepted the finality of personal death. By this act of abdication we have severed our relations with infinite solatus our selves from the Universe or if you like, from God. This loss of cosmic consciousness which you find expressed everywhere—in the cerebral character of modern poetry, painting, architecture and so on has led to the adoration of the new Ball : Society. I do not mean the worship of the totalitarian state, or even of the state as such : the real evil is the deification of society itself. Sociology, social science, social therapy, social integration, social what you have. Since we have accepted death as final, society, has been replacing the cosmos. Man has no longer any direct transactions with the universe, the stars, the meaning of life, all his cosmic transactions are monopolised and all his transcendental impulses absorbed by the fetish "society'. We do not talk any longer of homo-sapiens, of man, we talk of individual we do not aspire turned goodness and charity : we aspire for social interaction".

Arthur Koestler (in a Novel)

The tiny drops of water make the mighty oceans. If drops are not there, there would be no oceans. Similarly it is the small men and women, millions and millions that form the society. If they are not there, society and state cannot see the light of the day.

Tyrants

Drops of water are of course qualitatively different from those of human beings. The former are identical in every conceivable way we can think of. This is not so in case of men. Each and every individual is different from other individuals.

Men cannot be compared even with the ants too. The latter are more comfortably placed. They can live together, work together and over it enjoy in the performance of their duties whole heartedly. Their pattern of life had been stabilised long long time back. They do not imagine that they can rebel against that order in which they are placed. The concept of "rights" is not known to them. So they understand the priority of discipline even in the minutest details of their lives and that is all. This is how their minds are conditioned. There are a few other insects and animals that live and work together as a matter of routine. They do not feel disturbed if there is more work to do. They do not agitate if there is little food to eat.

This has not been the case with man. In history had been expressed ambition of many tyrants and megalomaniacs who had wished to reduce him to those levels of drops and ants but that had not worked for a long time till date.

Human Kind

People are tempted by so many things, namely wealth, land sex, children power and so on. They ponder over the state of those affairs in which they happen to live and then try to work out ways and means as to what they can do to improve upon them. They are quite often not satisfied with those conditions of life in which they are placed by those who happen to be in the authority. If their minds are reasonably developed, they ask strange questions. Why are their conditions unsatisfactory ?

What is their crime ? Why are all so many denials reserved for them ? If they turn angry or violent they may throw aside the imposed apparatus of law and order and clamour to achieve reasonable station in day to day life. It is not so with the ants. If men proceed with courage and wisdom, they would wrest those positions that are achievable.

This is a terrible world. Many shall have to come forward for moving the wheels of destiny. Law of life is to struggle. There is every reason to feel ashamed if we do not struggle against injustice. There is no reason to feel so in case of defeats, but here is another difficulty and that is psychic. It drives the defeated towards defeatism and then they refuse to examine the reasons of their failures. They ignore to study as to how these could have been averted and thus drift to living at low key believing that all struggling is of no use. It would not help them to mend their fortunes.

Common man, as he lives, is not an embodiment of self-control self-abnegation, self-surrender, self-devotion and so on. He is a bundle of a few virtues and some vices and foibles. He may not also be looking for achieving something extra-ordinary in his life. He is generally satisfied with marginal success in the struggles that life opens to him. His objectives are also limited. He is not ready to make colossal sacrifices for realising them. If he fails, he straightway rationalises that odds were heavy against him. So it was no good to break his head against the wall. Ultimately this kind of attitude does not result in the change in his life style. Material conditions are very important though he values many other things in his life too. Each and every individual has, his own likes and dislikes. He is cut out in a particular way.

Professionalism

In our times the wave of professionalism has taken over the human society. Many scientists, technologists, engineers, administrators, economists, managers etc, have ascended the scene and are handling the problems at various levels. They are equipped with specialised knowledge plus skills and as a result, their influence is being increasingly felt all round. With many positive influences this phenomenon has a dark side too. A chemist may know a lot about chemistry, but he is blank in economics, and say in many other areas of life, but he is a human being at the same time. His professional responsibilities are discharged very effectively by him and he may be identified as an eminent chemist, but as an individual he is more than that. This is the fate of our men and women of professions.They have no comprehensive view of life in totality which they are destined to lead as members of an advaned section of society.

Our Age

Our age is perhaps a flag station in the long journey of time. We are at once situated at the end point of a long past and at the beginning of an enormous future. There is nothing unusual about it except that we are living in it. We always matter most to ourselves. This caravan would not wait here for a long time and then moves on. In the process, we shall complete our lives' journey which is of very short duration. Mankind would live but men and women we see would disappear generation after generation leaving a few records behind. Most of their activities would go into oblivion. Many of those developments which occupy our attention area at the moment are of very little cousequence for the furture. All would not find place in the records of future history.

Society

The society should be open or closed is a matter of debate for the pandits of political theory. As a layman I feel and feel strongly that the over-all view of our present society which is considered an open one is disappointing. It is a pathetic specimen. There is no discipline, no order, no control and above all, people do not think in terms of setting up some standard in their performances. There is no plan, no scheme and no ideology that should have inspired them for acquiring the means of meaningful living. Science and technology are rendering significant services to the people. Production of all human necessities is increasing. People are consuming them more then ever in history. Society is however benignly open for those who are prospering quickly. For the rest it is either a blind alley or a battlefield.

People

People are generally confused. They are suffering in silence. They express their anger and dissatisfaction in so many ways but with no strong desire to change the order. Our present hardships would not disappear of their own. We have to struggle against them. As soon as people learn that they should stop lying down, collect their strength and organised their efforts' a movement would see the light of the day and from there far reaching consequences are bound to follow. Only then rulers would feel threatened. To begin with they would try to suppress the people's demonstrations of anger and dissatisfaction. The masters are very clever. They are well aware as to how far they could eoncede the demands of the people without jeopardising their own authority. They would not permit their rule being thwarted. They are organised. The entire State power is at their disposal. Above this, the talent of the society is at their command. Means of propaganda are also controlled by them. The news and views are modified to meet their needs. If the people are not adequately prepared their upsurge would be crushed. History is replete with such details that many of their past agitations had ended in fiasco. Truth may be on the side of people, but that is not enough. Organised power of the State strangulates it. Its so-called ultimate victory placed in the closed envelope to be opened in some distant future is of no use to the present generation of men and women.

Individual

What can a poor common man do in the given circumstances ? He feels all insecure, frustrated and disillusioned. He at times ponders over his insignificant life like that of a petty philosopher, as if he is just like that of a bird who flies from one branch of the tree to another, leaving no trace of its flight in the air. He does not create a pathway. This is how he completes his life story. Well, that is not enough. He has to prove his potential. Two options are open to him. He may withdraw from the struggle or join hands with those who are still fighting their ways. It depends upon his resolution. Certain early defeats are solemn teachers, but their intensity is at times severe that breaks the spirit of the man.

It is very fine to advise that people should re-examine their performances and discover the reasons of their failures and thereafter fresh attempts may be made. It has been observed that at times hardships of life are so shattering that reasoning in man fails to build up his courage. The inclination for fatalism which has been suppressed by him through serious efforts takes charge of his mind and that works as a straw to the drowning man.Much is said against it in all the books but only the wearer knows how the shoes pinches. If the hostile conditions continue indefinitely, that break the will of even the most powerful minds. Fatalism is then a relieving philosophy. It pacifies conflicting minds. Its reasoning may be refuted, its logic can be rejected, but its appeal cannot be denied. It helps the man to carry on.

State

We meet it as a reality. We experience its power and omnipotence. Individual submits to its authority. If he dares rebel against its orders, he is decimated. Well, if the individual is like that of Lenin or Gandhi, he would stand fast against its suppression. Then if he is killed, he goes down in history as a martyr. If he outwits other he takes control and then would use power for actualising his ambitions. Such individuals are unusual and uncommon.

Controllers of Modern State claim to stick to some kind of ideology or philosophy, but that is only the mask they wear. In reality, it is the institution of that class or a group of people who manage to seize it. What to say of creating a fair and just state in the real sense of the terms, the political theorists of the world have not yet been able to evolve a system even in theory which could have struck a right balance between the rights of an individual as against the authority of the State.

The issue is not just to serve a particular class or a caste or a region or a religious group of people. We are concerned with the welfare and progress of the entire human race. The character of the state is to be transformed to reach our level of expectations. It must respond to the urges of those men and women who are being treated as dumb driven cattle by the rulers of the times.

It is unfortunate to state that the scientific and technological progress is being used for strengthening the existing apparatus of the State. Most of the eminent scientists and technologists of the world are just petty jobseekers in the courts of those who are managing the affairs at the top. It is very seldom when some eminent scientist plucks the courage and asserts against the inhuman policies being pursued by his State. Such bold examples are very few.

The compulsions of physical existence are very powerful even for the best minds of the world. They are also required to sell their labour for earning their livelihood. The results of their hard work are seen in the arsenals of the world powers. Their use is controlled by the State authorities who happen to be mostly politicians. The decision making powers regarding the destiny of human race rests with them.

It is pity we have not been able to evolve a culture in which people should have been rewarded or awarded on the basis of their performances. If a surgeon spends ten hours in the operation theatre and saves a life from death, he hardly gets a mention in the press. As against him a meaningless speech of a political leader would occupy front pages of national dailies, since the State power is at his back.

8

CIVILISATIONAL CRISIS

"It is a sobering thought that we are a privileged generation not only because we may be the first to see the dawn of the third millenium after Christ, but because we may be the last generation of human beings to inherit this planet. Can we accept the second possibility as passive spectators and drift mindlessly towards disaster ? Can we acquiesce in a situation where one quarter of mankind is overfed and three quarters underfed, where millions suffer from obesity and overeating while hundreds of millions waste slowly away from malnutrition, stunted in body and mind ; where millions are over medicated, and hundreds of millions lack access even to elementary medical facilities ? Can we close our ears to the cry of the deprived and oppressed, while the world plunges on towards it rendezvous with the ultimate apocalypse ? If the answer to the questions is in the negative as it must be, then we have to move towards transition to a new, global consciousness which will enable us to survive in the global village which we now inhabit. We have to transit to complementarity in place of competition, convergence in place of conflict, holism in place of hedonism. We must heal the split within human psyche, we must gather the fragments of human consciousness and round them into a glowing whole, we must effect the transition to a new global consciousness to replace the present fractured and fragmented consciousness in the human race."

Dr. Karan Singh

We are told by great minds of our times that this age is passing through a civilisational crisis of a very serious magnitude. Changes are so quickly overtaking us that we are being caught unprepared and thus are failing to adjust with the new situations. In the circumstances we have lost the overall sense of direction. There are no correct pointers. We are therefore required to propose such ways and means that should help us to respond effectively in the given conditions.

Issues are getting confounded with the increasing implications. The idea appeals that there is a limit to which individual can stretch himself. He confronts so much of information. He has to pick and choose what part of it is useful to him. Since total data is not at his command, he cannot make objective assessment of the situation. What to say of achieving a mature view of things around, he can hardly know a part of totality. So his over all capabilities are always limited if not stunted, but the problems are growing gigantic.

This is a peculiar crisis. The chequered history of man confirms that he could have transformed many of his past ambitions into suitable ideals. The people could aspire for great achievements and for that they were ready to make sacrifices. They had not always been obsessed by the instinct of self-preservation. They could at times be capable of looking upward and sought the right expression for their personalities.

We can hope that they would rise to the occasion again for overcoming the present civilisational crisis. Man today is very much in need of such thoughts that may help him to believe that he is destined to overcome his problems if he determines to do so. That is why we say that Utopian streaks are required in his thought processes. The present status of our life is colourless, tasteless and odourless. We should therefore work out achievable ambitions and plan to convert the same into great causes to fight for. All our activities should be so pursued that results are also shown as scheduled. That would build up the reliability on those who are at work.

The psychic conditions of the people of our age are pathetic. These are to be reconditioned quickly even if we have to resort to some kind of strong indoctrination. We know there are opportunities but on self-scrutiny we doubt our possibilities and thus fail to act. We have nothing in our defence but to adhere to certain past positions with the belief of their being rightly ordained. We carry a lot of dead weight in our minds. We have to shed it if progress is our aim.

If timely action is not taken, the circumstances surrounding the present crisis would worsen still further. Human possibilities in material sense of the term have enormously increased over the years and with them our approach to the problems should have been modified. Here is, of course, a warning. Even a slight miscalculation on our part can misfire and we are not in a position to imagine the dire consequences. "To err is human" is a very old proverb and its correctness is not challenged even to-day but the consequences of future errors may be disastrous. Even then we have to act and grapple with the issues. Onward improvement of man and his society and state is absolutely necessary. We cannot hold up the process of transformation. It is to be made inevitable. If we do not take charge of our circumstances, efficiently, conditions would drift.

New Civilisation

Human knowledge has exploded over the years especially in the fields of science and technology. Now that is influencing our other areas of life, namely social, economic, political and even spiritual. At the moment this penetration may appear to be slow in our society but its tempo would increase in the years to come. By habit, people respect the popular norms of social, economic, political and religious life, but that may not continue in the years to come. People would look for better and more sophisticated arrangements of things around.

Gradually we are discovering ourselves afresh in so many ways. A question is begged by the changing conditions. Are we really more comfortable and better placed than our predecessors ? If our great grandparents come to life once again, would they feel jealous of our present conditions ? I would say, "Yes" on certain issues and "No" on others. Where light has increased, the darkness has not disappeared. It persists. New areas have been found where prompt actions are to be taken. New awareness is there, but it is not generating high hopes and confidence amongst the people. History cannot be created by those who are running after money or are involved in wresting musical chairs of power. They are petty minds. Small men. Inconsequential men. There is no confidence, no ability, no devotion, no firmness and no certainty in their thoughts and actions. We are in need of such manpower that understands our compulsions.

With the increasing uncertainties generated by the crisis of this civilisation, many of our energies are being sapped by real and imaginary fears. The knowledgeable are more hamletized and confused than common people. The former do not know how to proceed further. They are stuck up. The latter are not in a position to move since they need guidance and help. They may not be satisfied with the existing conditions, but are not ready to challenge them. Some of us have to take up the cudgels otherwise people in general would prefer to be left to themselves. For shaking their indifference and lethargy we have to raise task forces. They would bring these people out from the present stupor and suggest them new vistas of thoughts and hopes so that they could be directed towards new routines of living.

History certifies that the "survival of the fittest" had been the principal law that had shaped human destiny over the centuries. Times have changed now. Who is likely to survive in case of a nuclear warfare ? Who would be the fittest man then ? Odds are obviously very heavy. This is a big question mark that haunts our age. If human life has to continue, new directions for pushing it forward are to be discovered. New foundations are to be laid. The time old phenomenon of ruthless competitions shall have to compromise with that of cooperation at every level.

If efforts are made well in time, positive results would flow inevitably. If we refuse to read what is written on the future wall of history, we may either reach the end of total devastation or somewhere through trial and error. "We live in a highly competitive society," wrote S.I. Haya Kawa, "each of us trying to outdo the other in wealth, in popularity or social prestige in dress, in scholastic grades, a golf scores. As we read our daily papers, there is always news of conflict rather than of cooperation—conflict between labour and management, between rival corporations or movie shows, between rival political parties and nations. Over us all hangs the perpetual fear of another war even more unthinkably horrible than the last. One is often tempted to say that conflict, rather than cooperation is the great governing principal of life.

But what such a philosophy overlooks is that, despite all competition at the surface, there is a huge substratum of cooperation taken for granted that keeps the world going. The coordination of the efforts of engineers, actors, musicians, camera men, utilities companies, typists, programme directors, advertising agencies, writers and hundreds of others is required to put on a single television programme. Hundreds of thousands of persons cooperate in the production of motor cars, including suppliers and shippers of raw materials from different parts of the earth. Any organised business activity whatsoever is an elaborate act of cooperation, in which every individual worker contributes his share. A lock out or a strike is a withdrawal of cooperation, things are regarded as "back to normal" when cooperation is restored. We may indeed as individuals compete for jobs, but our function in the job we get is to contribute at the right time and place to that innumerable series of cooperative acts that eventually result in automobiles being manufactured, in cakes appearing at pastry shops, in department stores being able to serve their customers, in the trains and airlines running on schedule.

This network of cooperation we have created is intricate and complex, and it has been relatively effective. But because it rests so profoundly upon human agreement, it is also fragile and vulnerable." We have entered an era when it is to be strengthened from all sides. We have no other choice.

Search

In the past, human life was guided and moulded by religious prophets, powerful kings and reformers. From time to time they used to throw up a set of ideas for motivating people to to do something. In most of these historic developments, during the initial stages efforts were made to propagate simple, straightforward, clear and to the point values and duties.The people were then persuaded to adopt them. They were gradually convinced of their usefulness and had no reservations in following them. They accepted the new ideas and responsibilities enthusiastically.

There had been instances when such change over had been painful. People were at times found physically and psychically distressed. They did not wish to abandon their familiar environment. We are at the moment stuck up like them. Times are changing. Conditions are changing very fast. Old values and customs are failing to help us. Still we are not in a position to adjust with the new situations. Our esteem for many of the past values persists and that is leading to so many contradictions in our lives.

We are in need of such ideologies, systems and philosophies that may help us to meet the changing circumstances with courage, intelligence and sobriety. We may pick up such illustrious examples from the past and the present that strengthen our desire to acquire dynamic and positive conduct and then application of our minds for grappling with the issues otherwise we shall fail to confront the challenges to arise.

Common Man and Civilisation

Time has come to redefine the roles of many institutions around which human life revolves. The present norms of family, society, state and allied institutions should be redefined. New foundations of property relations may be laid. Existing ones are creating havoc. New programmes of National Education may be drawn up. Fresh lists of rights and responsibilities of the citizens are to be worked out. Who would do all this for common man ? The Heavens would not come to his help. He has to depend on his own self. He should try to know what others have got to say but at the same time must explain his own side of the case and then arrive at some decision.

Civilisations had never been raised by those who rolled in luxuries or had depended exclusively on the ideals of the past. The real creators are always those who cherish high ideals suitable to their times and have the will to suffer for their realisation. There are few amongst men and women who go to the gallows for some higher causes. Some of their records have come down to us. There are many others who had been crucified, but remain all unnoticed and unhonoured. They also worked for raising civilisations. For instance, we remember Shahjahan, the great Mughal emperor of India who got built the Taj at Agra but there were thousands and thousands of architects and workers who worked for it. History is silent about them.

Future

New epochal and constructive programmes would not be thrown up by the bureaucracy implanted by our rulers. The serious intellectual efforts are required from those who are pained but seized to do something positive. Here bookish knowledge would not meet their future yearnings. The useful ideas would strike only to those who are grappling with the problems to restructure the existing order of the society. Campaigns to actualise them would be launched thereafter.

With increasing complexities, what to say of a common man even intellectuals are feeling handicapped. A few cannot master the entire data for making the important decisions. Many of them shall have to sit together and form a "Think Thank". In the beginning those who are likely to participate in such activities would not be noticed by the Press or Radio or T.V. Yes a bang would come when certain startling results are thrown up by them on the surface of society. The solutions of our pressing problems like hunger, starvation, illiteracy, malnutrition and slums etc. would then be taken up.

9

GRAPPLING WITH THE PROBLEMS (PART I)

"Men will not receive the truth from their enemies, and it is very seldom offered to them by their friends..."

Alexis de Toqueville

"Men have a restless reaching out for ideals. The human individual has to work his evolution consciously and deliberately. He has to act responsibly and cooperate willingly with the purpose of evolution."

Dr. S. Radhakrishnan

New India would not be created by the debates in the Lok Sabha. "Pad-yatras" of the disgruntled leaders would not bring revolutions. Tours and speeches of the leaders would not help in banishing our poverty. The problems of millions and millions cannot be tackled just by such gimmicks. We are rather in urgent need of those bright young men and women who should be convinced that they are to think and act only for becoming the bricks of the plinth of future India. They would soon be forgotten. The historians would not record their services and sacrifices. If, at all, they do it say after some time, they would merely snub them for their failings and overlook the fact thay they were the path finders.

All our suggestions stated in these pages stand for maintaining peaceful environment. It is true that march of history can be accelerated by the use of violence and quick results can be obtained, but that would not last long. Bloodshed leaves its effects of far reaching consequences. Over it we are confronted with enormous possibilities of destruction. The entire human race can be decimated. Since the people can be persuaded, educated and indoctrinated for obtaining the desired results, we should invariably follow the routes of peace and non-violence in executing our programmes. Correct homeopathic treatment of a disease is much better than that of a surgical operation advised by allopaths. Wars have become extremely disastrous. Thousand and lakhs of people are killed for no cogent reasons. When an individual dies, a son dies. A brother dies. A husband dies. A father dies. A friend dies. An institution dies. A world dies. At whatever age he passes away, he could have lived for some more time. If millions and millions like him are killed, we may imagine the loss.

Nation Building

Building of Nation State in a country of the size of India is a huge task. Our people are divided on so many scores. They have a long history in which they had been acquiring varying loyalties. It is true that individuals fight as organised forces but from the back parts of their minds loyalties provide them support and that create personalities out of them, so they organise themselves in a particular order. Their heads are seldom at work. Their actions are largely determined by the messages from their hearts. Here reasons are less important and emotions are consequential. Our primary task is therefore, to bring the heads and hearts of the people closer by pursuading them around some humanistic ideology. They are to organise themselves against hunger, malnutrition, illiteracy, backwardness, unemployment and so on. Men and women living in neighbouring and distant territories or belonging to different religions and caste denominations are not their real enemies. Our struggles are against those social, economic and political evils that make the lives of common people miserable.

Under the present state of affairs, it would be naive to predict that forces of the national unification would win hands down. Diversities in the national life fail to accord prestigious position to the ideal of National Unity. The workable synthesis is not in sight. It is to be evolved.

Enlightened Self-Interest

Common people are to be educated about their enlightened self interest. They are even to be indoctrinated that they should not remain idle spectators of the ups and downs of the present history that is unfolding itself all over the world. It is influencing their present and future in so many ways. If their interests are being trampled, they have to stand up as crusaders.

Mercenaries

How are we to raise an epochal movement ? A few meaningful programmes are to be proposed. Masses are to be drawn out of their homes for building dams, long roads, powerful bridges, hospitals, schools, and a huge network of small and big industiral units wherever possible all over the counry. Informal education for strengthening community feeling is to be spread on warfooting. That must obviously include short term educational programmes for rapid agricultural and industrial progress. People's faith in seeking mercenary positions as against the voluntary work is to be shaken by acknowledging the preformance of dedicated work. We have no national wage structure at the moment. We have no yardsticks to disburse payments against the actual performance of work. It is the solemn function of Press as well as of the Government to highlight the performance of voluntary agencies. Selfless work does not get its due under the present state of affairs. Voluntary agencies and their workers may appear to be men of straw, but they are straws of intellect, initiative, selflessness, comprehensive integrity, competence and above all of love. All great people who have contributed for the uplift and progress of human race were associated with of some such agencies.

People are generally self-centred. They are to be prepared for acquiring new attitudes. At the moment they are more interested in increased wages but less work and low production. How can we fight against poverty if such trends are not curbed. This is a national dilemma today. It is not understood as to how such conduct would help the poor and the vanquished. The underfed and undernourished are not to locate their enemies amongst the rich only.

It is complained that common people are miserly, calculating and least sacrificing. They refuse to ascend. They fail to realise as to where their real interests are lying. They do nct res ond to the calls given by well meaning and sincere comrades. The difficulty is that appeals for working hard are not in accordance with their present thought-constructs. It has been observed that under such depressing conditions many sincere and well meaning idealists abandon their pursuits and quietly withdraw to other professions leaving the futurity of the people to those who are unconcerned with the issues.

New Leaf of Life

A peculiar situation has arisen. The so-called utopians or mini prophets are no longer respected in public life. This has a serious side effect, the mankind has seriously been impoverished in the ethical domain. We are facing its consequences. We look forward for good neighbours, well meaning teachers, affectionate bank clerks, honest officials, responsible physicians sympathetic police constables and so on. They are nowhere available. Where have they all disappeared ? The overall situation is so chaotic. We have no restraints over ourselves but we expect others to be all considerate. This is strange.

The over emphasis on material considerations has damaged the finer fibres of modern human life, It would not be out of place to mention here that certain sound cultural values amongst the people were cultivated with great efforts over centuries. Late Dr. Eric Fromn the famous American psycho-analyst had said some where "That in a world in which there are no values except success, no norms except the commandments to increase production and consumption endlessly, a society which men change themselves completely to manipulated tasks and to public opinion that in such a world a need arises to find again meaning to life and a longing becomes felt for some kind of religious renaissance. In public life we see no hope. In literature we read depressing details. Newspapers are full of quarrels, competitions, conflicts etc. Cinema stands for rape, violence and what not. Schools are either without teachers or furniture. University life is diseased in so many ways. Where should we go for locating the sun of optimism ? Scientific approach does not help much since it is silent on such issues. Where are those fountains where people should drink deep and deep for wresting hope and confidence ? Frantic search has well begun in the certain quarters of the world to weave new order of life. We should not lag behind. We are rather a nation that has a record of leading in such matters. "The political and economic systems" wrote late Buckminister Fuller, "and political and eeonomic leaders of humanity are not in final examination, it is the integrity of each individual human that is in final examination. On personal integrity hangs humanity's fate. You can deceive others you can deceive your brainself, but you cannot deceive your mind-self [for mind deals, only in the discovery of truth and the interrelationship of all the truths. The cosmic laws with which mind deals are non-corruptible,"

Cooperation

The issues are so large and tasks so formidable that no single man can achieve much. Conditions are much complicated. So he shall have either to cooperate or get collectivised by others. The third alternative is his extinction. The most suitable and convenient course available to him is to work in cooperation with others. Doubts can be raised over it also. We can refute a proposition just by refusing it, but that is not the way of reaching a workable solution.

Fate

In India, a few years ago, an individual could quietly bank upon the myth of fate for meeting the oddities and adversities of his life. That is not so today. He knows that life is no longer a gamble in absolute terms. There are at once so many uncertainties as well as possibilities, that come in his way. Well it is the solemn duty of each and every individual to work out his plans throughly and ensure that possibilities of errors are minimised. These cannot of course be ruled out in their entirety. There are many who put in the best of their efforts, but fail to reach their goal. They are lost in the way. Under the circumstances fatalism is very comforting philosophy to them. It is a straw for a drowning man. It would save him from total collapse. The dilemma is that there are many lazy coward and indifferent people who turn fatalists without putting up a bitter fight. They refuse to struggle for discovering their best and take shelter under shade of fatalism. In the process they are robbed of their will to fight. Their dynamism wears out. Their initiative disappears. We need bull dog determination in fighting out our way. Opportunities are few and we are too many to seek. Let us try our level best.

Birth Rate

We hope that in the years to come birth rate of Indian children would considerably decline. People, in general, woud realise that more children would not help them to break the shackles of poverty. All efforts to motivate people in this respect, should be intensified.

Environment

Efforts are to be made that natural environment are preserved to the extent possible. For that artificial forestation would pick up. We are in need of a nation-wide movement for preserving environment. Trees and plants are our friends. All other animals are our relatives. It should be the solemn duty of each and every individual to grow trees and plants and love animals to the extent possible.

Early Efforts

Here is an opportunity for all political and social organisations to help the people out. It may be recalled that a few cooperative movements had been launched in India from time to time a few years back, but these could not execute the tasks assigned to them. People had no experience of their management. At times initial attempts do not produce desired results since so many details in respect of overall preformance could not be anticipated and that had carried the boat of the past cooperatives to rough waters, but this does not mean that our future efforts would not succeed also. Perhaps people were not adequately motivated then. They fumbled. The past traditions and practices had strongly occupied their consciousness for which they could not correctly appreciate the essence of the new experiment of cooperative movements. They had to unlearn so many things. We may take stock of the total situation once again and launch new cooperative movements.

Education for Unlearning

The process of unlearning is, in fact, a new phenomenon of modern education. We are not accustomed for such an effort of acquiring knowledge. It is entirely a different kind of orientation. People are to be brought out from the routine world of their past to the present times. They are by and large not open minded. Their views are rigid. They refuse to admit that their prevailing procedures would not respond to their emergent needs. Correct Education should help men and women to grow. They should be in a position to evaluate their activities thoroughly and plan of making them more useful and helpful. It must inspire them to live by working hard coupled with honesty. It should wipe out their present complacency.

All accomplishments of the individuals would be of little use if they do not align their efforts with the overall developments of the society. This is not to be examined in terms of economics alone. Our value systems had of course laid considerable emphasis on many aspects of life but somehow we have gone astray. Scholars of political theory, economists of various schools, social thinkers of all varieties, psychologists, anthropologists and others should from a think-thank to work out the fresh details as to how the functions of the state, needs of the society, and the requirements of the individuals are integrated with maximum advantage to those who form poorest strata of the society. Computers may also be pressed into service for processing the information.

A new global thinking may seize the minds of those who would matter. If the world resources are exhausted ruthlessly, it would affect the futurity of entire mankind. These would dwindle and the people may then be crushed under the weight of penury. The world is not to be reduced to the "House of the dead". Special care is to be taken. We are very close to a very prosperous age, provided we can achieve an under standing of ecological interdependence of this earth and necessity of abandoning those habits that lead to mismanagement of resources. So it is the solemn duty of all educational institutions to advocate and work for the preservation of the natural resources of this earth to the extent it is possible. Along with the ardent desire for world peace, minimum use of natural resources should also find place in the programmes of the important political parties. This is must.

Role of Formal Education

More importance should be accorded to informal education. The patronage to formal education may be reduced at least for some time. A great revolution is imperative in this respect. For instance, whatever is cultivated at religious places or at political platform is the process of informal education. It goes too far in the working of the human conduct. The impressions so received on the minds of the people are indelible. We can feel their impact amongst millions and millions.

On the other hand, over all state of formal education is disappointing. Its framework is clumsy and irrelevant. Whatever little revision has been effected through the New Education policy, it would not achieve much since the teaching community is not ready to play a positive role for making procedural changes as instruments of regeneration of the society. It is rather all absorbed in petty personal gains.

Here some revolutionary steps are to be taken. Only then the break up with the past structures of the educational system is possible. Our primary interest is to rebuild future of the taught and not to assure security of employment and higher wages to the teaching staff. What is most important is being shelved and side issues are engaging full attention. What to say of revising system throughly there is no dearth of unfits and misfits in our teaching faculties. If the students are not provided constructive ideas to build a modernised society, all other efforts would take us nowhere.

10

GRAPPLING WITH THE CRISIS (PART II)

"Life continuously alters the environment, and the altered environment in turn alters the potentials, realities and challenges of life. Environment embrace a complex of non simultaneously occurring but omni integrating mutations of human's external, only by invention-realised metabolic-regeneration organisms which we think and speak of as industrialisation''

R. Buckminister Fuller

We need not imply go to the hoary past for picking up the threads to resurrect modern India. The year 1947 may be treated as an important watershed. The changes that have been affected thereafter should be dispassionately examined. That would enlighten us as to why we could not proceed as per the expectations of Gandhiji and others. We should investigate our failures. Nehru and most of his colleagues were well-meaning but the difficulty with them had been that they were reluctant to take critical and hard decisions and preferred soft options so that the decadant framework of the Indian society they inherited did not collapse in such a manner that they would have failed to take charge of the unforeseen difficult conditions. They belived that people would not welcome revolutionary changes. In fact, they had played safely.

Discipline

How can we progress rapidly when indifference and complacency are ruling large over the minds of the people ? First of all they are to be inspired. We may speak against the discipline imposed by the state but if individuals persistently refuse to acknowledge their responsibilities, what should be done by the state ? It would be an ideal state of affairs if individual opts for self-discipline, but if such lofty objective does not appear to be realisable, something is to be done for the society. We are not to write books on the subject rather face the issues in the real life.

Persuasive techniques may be tried. These have reasonable possibilities to succeed, but it is not sure that expected results would be obtained. Men and Women would peruse over them and then apply their minds whether their expectations could be met by their adaptation. Their response generally depends upon the impressions they would gather for their personal benefits. There are many who would take it that discipline would mean their suppression. How can they accept it ? Here it is very important to point out that self-discipline should at least be displayed by those who are at the helm of affairs. They must prove it beyond doubt that they are its embodiments. Their sterling example would certainly be a great source of inspiration to others.

Hunger

The principal objective before us is to achieve freedom from hunger and other immediate human needs to achieve modest standard of living for those who are living just slightly above and all below poverty line. Let us confess that our poverty is bottomless. It is horrible in many parts of the countryside. Individual, society and state shall have to work together with single mindedness and eradicate it. What comes in the way to achieve this simple end is to be faced with courage. Major responsibility in this respect lies with the organised sections of working classes of agricultural and industrial worlds. They are to help those who are below them. If they fail to rise to the occasion, they have no face to ask others to do the needful. These poverty stricken people who live on subsistence level are their kiths and kins.

Government

Government must set its house in order. We expect it to be an ideal institution. We should not find any slackness in its performance. Whatever tasks are assigned to any of its department that should be implemented in letter and spirit. Each and every employee of the Government is required to justify his identity by virtue of his output of work. If high ranking designations are given and fat salaries paid for non-performance, people are bound to agitate against all this. The leadership should take objective stock of the situation and do the needful. It, of course, goes without saying that if the government is supposed to be an ideal employer, the same idealism must pulsate amongst the employees. There is a serious charge that all those employees who come into contact with public in general, are corrupt through and through. It is a subject over which volumes could be devoted.

Working Class

The organised working class has been eating into the vitals of the society whereas a large segment of the latter is underfed, undernourished, badly housed and ill clad. The overall level of our industrial production is much less than that of productivity, but at the same time wages of the workers are increasing. Efficiency is lying wounded all over the country. Here it is difficult to apportion blame on some particular group or agency. We cannot exactly say who is eating whom. It however, goes without saying that the leaders of the organised working class are not answerable or accountable to the society. They just serve the interests of small sections i.e. the trade unions of the workers. Where private sector is involved, the capitalists are blamed for taking away exhorbitant profits but where are the profits of public sector? Enormous funds were invested over the years. These were raised by the people of India not for serving the interests of the staff or the management deployed therein.

On one side we have Army Jawans defending the frontiers of the country at the highest possible altitudes of the world. Every minute of their lives is in peril. On the other hand, we have a fast growing number of organised workers in all categories and grades both in public and private sectors with pathetically very low level of production. If country is really to be build up, some rationale is to be worked out. It is no good shouting slogans against the capitalists or the Government. It should also be examined as to what exactly our Trade Unions are also doing. Well, they cannot be treated all the time as the most aggrieved section of our society. Do they ever bother to realise that with the increased wages and better equipment being made available to them, their production should also go up proportionately ? What have their leaders to say in this regard ? It is high time that Government should open a few educational institutes where short-term courses for the working classes be introduced. Group discussions and seminars should also be conducted for educating them as to what exactly should be achieved by them under the given conditions. If they are left to themselves, no good results are likely to emerge. If the present appeasement policies are followed for a long time, their results would be disastrous.

Trade Union activities

Bureaucrats, professors of Universities, scholars and other eminent men from different professions sit together, eat, drink discuss and disperse. Thereafter a press report appears describing their findings. This is not the way of educating those who are required to show results. The activities of our Trade Unions might have helped a sizable number of our workers, but society as a whole has not been benefited by their agitations or even by their higher wages. National resources are largely proceeding to the coffers of the management and staff. These are not being collected in the form of capital for further investment in various productive activities of the society. We have very limited resources. Over it, these are not being judiciously put to use. How would our poverty disappear under these conditions ?

Merit

Wages should be determined by performance and not by those agreements arrived at by the concerned under threats or otherwise. The policies that have been evolved over the years undoubtedly provide security of jobs to the workers but does not encourage them to outshine. So they do not aspire for awards or rewards. It is enough for them that their jobs are protected even if their performance is unsatisfactory. Had they felt the gravity of the situation, we are confronting at the moment, our modern history would have been written differently. Our overall progress would have been enviable. In life, it is better to be late than never. Even at this stage if correct steps are taken, we shall enter a new era and raise a great civilisation. The wisdom of thousands of years acquired through slow process of absorption is in the back yards of our minds. Even today as human material. Japanese are in no way superior to Indians, but there is a world of difference between our performances and theirs. What prompts Japanese to work hard is their competitive spirit, and strong determination to build up their nation. If they can do wonders by dint of their hard work, we are also capable of doing the same.

Future Revolutions

Each age has its own compulsions. Future revolutions would not merely be political. These may transcend the class character and involve the entire human kind. Their essentials would be broadly humanistic. Unusual efforts would be made for sorting out those issues which plague our lives. Some of the past traditions are so fast that we fail to come out of their influences and refuse to see things objectively. There are many darwbacks in Municipal laws and more so in International Law. Time has come that we should examine international relations and propose more reasonable and workable arrangements amongst the Nation states. Many of the barbaric laws of the Medieval age which have divided human race into strict territories are to be modified.

Many new institutions for making the state and society more useful and benevolent are to be floated. With that, certain new social, political, economic and cultural trends would emerge. In the process, the foundations of new civilisation would be laid. Well, even then, there would be no dearth of unscrupulous people who would try to sidetrack the issues. They have always been there. Strict watch would be required to keep them in check.

For instance, "Sati" is a social evil. We all condemn it but it is not such an evil that is widely prevailing all over the country and for that we should not make it a life and death issue. We should rather fight against the real evils that have plagued our social life. One of them is the plight of widows and even other women in our families. There is "dowry system". Then burning of "Brides". "Early marriages" and so on. The crusaders should come forward with courage and fight against them. They are to persuade people to pick up the cudgels for getting conditions straight even if it imperils their privileges. It leaves a very healthy effect on others if we forego our traditional rights and stand in queue with those who are under privileged.

We see the results of the centuries old oppression over women and this has been bequeathed to us in the form of honourable traditions. Those who are benefited by their perpetuation generally uphold them for personal reasons. They so champion the cause of their interests as if these were divinely ordained. Others are helpless. They are left to submit. Iron chains are required to tie down the beasts and of course for criminals amongst men. Chains of traditions and usage are strong enough for the common man.

Constitution

Time has come that we should reconsider some part of our Constitution. We have to ensure that it helps us in strengthening and uniting our people. "Right to work" should be deleted from "Directive Principles and included in. "Fundamental Rights". We happen to live in a more enlightened era than that of fifth decade of this century. People are more aware of their rights now. The traditional respect for constitutional or other authorities is declining. This is a serious development. Violence has acquired greater appeal than ever.

We do not mean to underestimate the role of our founding fathers who drafted our Constitution. They kept their own time in view. They were also perhaps conscious of history, but all that had followed in these four decades could not have been visualised by them. They, however, did not mean to prepare a document which should not have been revised under new conditions. Our social, political, and economic conditions are changing very fast. Our aspirations are also different today. Constitution is to be revised in such a manner that it helps us in responding to emerging challenges with maturity.

Regionalism

Of late, we have noticed that many regional parties have sprung on the national firmament with a bang. Most of All India Parties that had been operating over the national scene for a long time appear to be sick and diseased. These are neither attracting talent nor the masses. They have past, but no present. Their future appears to be bleak. This is a serious development. We have to take suitable steps that our polity is not threatened or destabilised.

There is not dearth of enemies around who would very much like India fragmented. The unity of the country is to be preserved at all costs. So far as our Constitution is concerned, it acknowledges the aspirations of those who were fighting against the foreign rule. They had a particular concept of Unity in their minds. With the passage of time our needs have undergone a sea change. The leadership of the freedom movement could not anticipate that the formation of linguistic states could have jeopardised the Unity of the country. They firmly believed that all Indian languages had worked for arousing the national consciousness during the freedom movement and these would strengthen the bonds of national unity if given support after independence in the year 1947. The results are before us. The principle of creating linguistic States has proved a grievous mistake. We have to acknowledge it and make amendments. We are all respectful to our great leaders of modern age. We do not mean to find fault with their wisdom, but if some of their idea has been found incorrect, we should rectify the same.

11

GRAPPLING WITH THE CRISIS (PART III)

Hope, superior to fear, is neither passive like the latter, nor locked into nothingness. The emotion of hope goes out of itself, make people broad instead of confining them, cannot know nearly enough of what it is that makes them worldly aimed of what way be allied to them outwardly. The work of this emotion requires people who turn themselves actively into what is becoming to which they themselves belong. It will not tolerate a dog's life which feels itself only passively drawn into. What is, which is not seen through even wretchedly recognised. The work against anxiety about life and the machinations of fears is that against its creators, who are for the most part easily to identify, and it looks in the world itself richly people have always dreamed of this, dreamed of better life that might be possible. Everybody's life is pervaded by day dreams ; one part of which is just stale, even enervating escapism, even booty for swindlers, but another part is provocative, is not content just to accept the bad which exists, does not accept renunciation. This other part has hoping at its core, and is teachable. It can be extricated from the unregulated day dream and from its shy misuse, can he activated undimmed. Nobody has ever lived without day dreams, but it is a question of knowing them deeper and deeper and in this way keeping them trained unerringly, usefully, or what is right. Let the day dreams grow even further, since this means they are enriching themselves around the sober glance, not in the sense of cloggings but of becoming clear. Not in the sense of merely contemplative reasons which take things as they are and as they stand, but of participating reason which takes them as they go and therefore also as they could go better. Then let the day dreams grow really further, that is clearer, less random, more clearly understood and more mediated with the course of things. So that the wheat which is trying to ripen can be encouraged to grow and be harvested."

Enst Block

We should not stuff our minds with the text book ideologies. All out efforts are to be made to discover what is useful to our people. Others may perhaps help us materially if we are really starving, but they would think for our difficulties as seriously as we do is doubtful. We need not submit to those ideologies at least that have never kept our real conditions in view. Things are not all black or white. There are so many shades within these two colours. Still some position is to be chosen with the best of our ability. Alvin Toffler a renowned American thinker and writer of our times says, "In a world governed by absolute political dogmas in which terms like 'left wing, "righ wing" "liberal", "conservative" are still bandied about freely as though rich in meaning. It is refreshing to come upon a new idea that cannot be put into a convenient ideological cubby hole". The die hard theorists would never respond warmly to this view. Open minds, and broad visions are required for tackling the problems that confront us. What to say of domocratic world, even communist states are being pushed towards more and more liberalisation. Well, there are no short cuts to the path of progress. Total involvement of the people is imperative if certain Herculean tasks are to be performed. Whenever some new programme is launched it must be in the mind of leadership whether people would really feel enthused. It must click. They await the sincere calls of selfless leaders and friends.

Gandhiji

If the champions of New movement are sincere, that would excite and encourage people to come out whole heartedly in its support. They may ask inconvenient questions in the beginning but truth and sincerity would ultimately matter. The position of Gandhiji was abundantly clear to the people before he had returned from South Africa. He could straight away start his experiments for awakening the people socially, politically, economically, spiritually, and even morally.

Like all great leaders of all times, he did not know in the initial stage whether he would succeed. Still he pursued his activities tirelessly. His approach was multi dimensional. He rightly felt the pulse of the people and acted with the best of his intentions. He did not mind confessing his mistakes and that did not adversely affect his image.

Time has marched on but our people continue to be more same and less different in so many ways although they have been influenced by many important forces of modern history. Future Gandhis shall have to locate suitable issues for new beginnings. They are not just to imitate this master mind of the century rather make their own assessment of the conditions and throw up their programmes which should be executed. That is possible if they throw their own 'I's apart and become all integrated, 'with others'.

Many religious, social and cultural values of the rural India are still in tact. If people over there are approached for the changes in their life-styles, epochal changes would begin. For instance, new beginning may be made for agitating on the point "work for every body." Many other suggestions are scattered at different pages of this work. These may be further examined, modified and then brought to the masses for implementation. That would gradually open the possibilities for new social economic, political and cultural order. New thinking would drive to more constructive activities. Let us call a spade a spade. We have no dearth of such scholars and thinkers who are adept in complicating the matters. Our people have simple minds. If a good idea provides a jerk to their cerebrals, they would accept it straight away.

Present Conditions

In the past, the options for "Reconstruction" of the societies were few and the resources were also limited, but in our times where magnitude of problems had increased the number of new possibilities has also multiplied. Opportunities are also many. The people are required to seize them. Well, dangers are undoubtedly more than ever before, but that should not frighten the leadership and the people. This is implied in the present conditions. It cannot be helped.

Priorities

There are many issues that deserve immediate attention. Decisions regarding them should be made accordingly. We should face all facts squarely. If sensitive matters over which quick decisions are required, are unnecessarily postponed, that would augment the complications. Timely actions are, therefore, absolutely necessary. What exactly should be done cannot be understood from the broad generalisations that we are making. We have experts who draw the plans, but that is not enough. We are to throw up such men and women who are committed to see that plans are executed. They would live and die for it. That determination is not there. People could go to the gallows for achieving political independence, but they are not ready to do so for executing social and economic programmes being given to them. They perhaps see no romance in their implementation. That tempo is to be generated. Those who wish to play safe would cut no ice. Only those men and women are to come forward who mean to relieve the sufferings of the strangers and share their sorrows quietly.

New Vistas

According to Milovan Djilas a great writer and leader from Yogoslavia, "Ours is only one of the ways of life, that have been and that will be, that they who came before us know and those who came after us will know. To happen that way ever each time is to live, to ereate one's own world. Hence comes the irresistible charm of digging of the past and dreaming of the future". Time has come to see beyond the theoretical mountains of Marxism, Leninism, Gandhism, Nehruism and so on. New peaks are to be located and conquered.

All our problems do not revolve around economics and politics. In the twentieth century many other areas relating to human life have come to light and due attention is to be given to them for making it purposeful. Their findings are to be studied and remedial actions for our problems proposed. Many details of "New Knowledge" are to be grasped so that more correct solutions could be thrown up. We shall have to penetrate into the worlds of psychology, anthropology, and sociology and then integrate their findings in our thought processes.

Our Times

There is nothing to emulate from the present day political, cultural and ethical life. Most of the institutions are decaying. The situation is not static. It is drifting. Conditions are fluid. Corruption is rampant even at the highest echelons of power. If incidently some positive and constructive steps are taken, that generates surprise. These are unusual happenings. If we find some organisation working on certain principles, we cannot help adoring those who are deployed therein. The irony is many of the present day evils are neither denied nor decried. Those who are required to weed them out do not express their helplessness in this regard rather offer plausible reasons that these would remain, as something inescapable. This approach is obviously an indirect support for perpetuating decline and ruin of decent life.

People become important national leaders over night just by wearing milk-white Khaddi and through certain political manipulations, otherwise there is nothing ennobling in their lives. After all, how does it happen ? This was not the state of affairs forty or fifty years ago. We must find out reasons for permitting such developments. It is true that man is not born criminal, but it does not suggest that we should permit crime to grow and all steps are to be taken for its eradication through all possible means. The pity is that we are becoming specialists in rationalising the increasing influences of evils. Instead of pledging to fight against them we have become their humble apologists. In our long and chequered history we have suffered enormously on account of pessimism, hopelessness and nothingness preached by our religious stalwarts. Let us not seal our future on the advice of the apologists of evils and crimes.

Women

Over the years the social and economic status of women has

marginally improved in our society but much remains to be done. The birth of a female child is still considered a misfortune both in rural and urban world of India. Of late, things have slightly changed in the cities but that is not so all over. Something should be done to awaken the woman-power settled in far flung areas in the country for organising itself. Women form the half of our total population.

Among the women there are millions and millions long oppressed and suppressed by their parents, brothers, then by husbands and finally by sons and others. As soon they realise injustice under which they had been destined to live over centuries was the result of man's misuse and abuse of his physical superiority, they would move the heavens. They have to fight against this time old ugliness, darkness, backwardness, and injustice. That would be a more serious revolution of future times than many we have read in the books of history. Our women organisations are still in their infancy. Their programmes cater the needs of the few ladies of higher social strata living in the cities. A bright future awaits those leaders who would strike in this direction. They would grapple with the realities. Conditions are bound to change and these would not wait. Right helping hand would bring encouraging fruits.

It is the solemn duty of the State to direct mass media for increasing the general awareness of the people in this respect. Small task forces should also be raised from the intelligent urban men and women who should work amongst their rural counterparts. The latter are in very large number who live under the influences of old beliefs and values the most of which are outdated. They would not change over night. What is possible in the given circumstances should be focussed. This is inherent in the situation and for that we shall have to proceed dialectically to actualise our objectives. The programmes of door to door informal education would revolutionise the thought constructs of our people aud provide them new vision of life.

A new era would soon begn. People would also look for new ambitions. Time may come in their lives when they no longer depend on old props and switch over to the process of modernisation. They would soon set aside their fears and superstitions that dominate their heads, hearts and bodies.

At the moment, they are scared and do not feel anxious as to when and how the wheels of history are to be moved. Voluntary organisations should rise to the occasion. Some achievement in this direction would bring commendable results in near future. Those who are concerned with shaping future history should not remain all absorbed in pondering over the problems of a small section of womanhood living in the urban world. They have to come out and set their camps at odd places in the unknown rural world and start interaction with the woman folk there.

A few Stand

Attention of the people is to be directed on something better and higher. Many negative forces are well entrenched and these would always produce fears, anxieties and frustrations and that would thwart the efforts to march on. Mankind has been fortunate in one respect at least i.e. some people could at times see the light of the day for directing the history. Unfortunately their number has been very small. They had formed the vanguard. History has, of course, been cruel to many of them since it does not acknowledge the services of everybody. So many of them had been crushed unmarked. This would continue, but that should not dishearten those who have willed to do something. In the prophetic words of Ethal Rosenberg the famous U.S. Scientist.

Earth shall smile, my sons, shall smile,
And green, on our resting place.
The killings and, the world rejoice,
In brotherhood and Peace.
Work and building sons and build,
A monument to live and joy.
To human worth, to faith we kept,
For you my sons, for you.

Elite to note

For instance, we expect that our physicians should be Utopians and humanists. They should not migrate from our country and work amongst our people. Over it, they should not stick to the cities for improving their professional prospects and rather settle in the countryside. They must have the privelege of working amongst their people. It is argued that their education could have been possible through their society, so it is obligatory on their part to look after the sick within it as their first priority.

We need not feel shy of advising on the similar lines to our ministers, governors, bureaucrats, professors, and others. They are also the products of the society and have been raised to high positions by it. They should also increase their contacts with the people in rural India, Our prospective members of Parliament go to the far flung constituencies only when the election campaigns are in full swing. Once they are elected or defeated, they abandon their voters and return to their normal world which is a highly blessed order. Chinese have sent their educated people to the rural side of their country for changing environment of their village to modernity. We organise debates or seminars to this effect and fail to realise our objectives. Difficult and hard decisions are not easily executed in our "open society".

Instead of building up a new India, our elected and selected men and women in the present times are more absorbed in building up themselves. Real India is not there in their waking lives. If she is there in their dreams, we do not know.

Task Force

If we succeed in founding task forces of a new thousand selfless and trained workers, our people would be helped. Persuasion is a slow technique of educating people but it leaves enduring influences. These are felt in the lives of the people. They respond. They do not remain indifferent to what is explained to them and that too in the light of their interests. Time is not far when they become activists of the mighty movements and force the depressing conditions to disappear. With that, new history would begin.

12

GRAPPLING WITH THE CRISIS (PART IV)

"Great ideas come into the world as gently as doves. Perhaps, then, if we listen attentively, we shall hear, amid the uproar of empires and nations, a faint flutter of wings, the gentle stirrings of life and hope. Some will say that this hope lies in nation, others in a man. I believe, rather that it is awakened, revived, nourished, by millions of solitary individuals whose deeds and works every day negate frontiers and the crudest implications of history...Each and every man or the foundation of his own sufferings and joys builds for all."

Albert Camus

Till now the fruits of our liberation had been the prerogative of a few. For that, rulers need not be proud of their performance. Their first priority had been to remain in power. Other things could have waited for them. Whenever they talk of peace, and that does not sound genuine, their emphasis on law and order is for maintaining status quo so that their dominance may continue, but it is doubtful whether this state of affairs would last long. Bells are ringing. We hear them. Unfortunately many amongst it the ruling class are hard of hearing. The masses would be soon on move. They wish that their plight should change. It is not an effort for destabilisation in the real sense of the term still this order is to be changed. There is no other go.

It Gandhi is not on the scene, some lesser man may come forward and share the awaiting responsibilities. Even if, he perishes in the process he would be setting a few milestones in right direction. Gandhi ji had many predecessors, who wished India to become free. They cleared many forks scattered on the paths of history and finally he succeeded in realising his political objectives in the year 1947. At his instance the power was taken over by Nehru. The latter was incidently cut out differently. Prof. Bimal Prasad says, "Nehru in contrast was noted for his modern, scientific outlook and wanted to make India a fully modernised country in every sense of the large scale industrialisation and extensive application of science and technology." In fact, Nehru had all admiration for Gandhiji, but there was no love lost for Gandhism. After Gandhiji's death, the known Gandhians had never approved policies being followed by Nehru but they were not in a position to evolve Gandhian thought further. Times had changed, new ideas and ideals should have come forth for meeting new challenges.

Most of the Gandhians were unable to understand the confusion being generated by the rise of hunger for political power. Now different tasks were to be attended to. They did not aspire to seize power since they suffered from the complex that it would corrupt them. They could not creatively operate in the changed conditions. Another leader of great stature like that of Gandhi was required for meeting the challenge. Marx had a successor in Lenin but that had not so happened in case of Gandhi Ji so far. This is still awaited. What to say of individuals, there are some political parties that claim to have followed Gandhism for reconstructing India, but they have no future programmes that could be certified as robust and healthy extensions of the Gandhian philosophy. Only lip service is done to this great leader for attracting votes in the elections. A great philosophy is not for such a mean objective. It is like a living stream of thought that flows through times changing forms and contents and still growing richer in substance. Its sameness does not rest as to how much we quote it rather in the continuity of its movement and its over all direction. It should strike as an organic whole, work in constant movement and not as something static.

Saints and Sadhus

We have a tradition of saints and sadhus travelling all

over the land from one place to another. In the past when the means of transport were negligible but spiritual messages were to be spread these religious men used to move from one place to another for propagating religious thought. There are Sadhus of certain sects even to-day who do not stay at one place for more than three days. We are in need of such cadres that should operate in the far flung areas of the country. Their messages are obviously to be different in subject matter but the routine of going from village is to be same.

Now no areas of the country are extremely difficult to reach and increasing facilities for communication are also available, but we have no selfless workers in any organisation who may come forward. If efforts are made as proposed, we would not simply reach the grassroots level of our people rather come to know much more about their real conditions. The information that we have at the moment is short, incomplete, incorrect and lopsided. We happen to live in a computer age. If more information is at our command, better programmes can be chalked only.

We have to found new organisations and institutions for throwing up social and political workers of high integrity and sound calibre. It is a hard nut to crack. There is no yearning to do something unusual amongst our young people. They do not feel inspired for undertaking that work which is not remunerative. The dream of leading a better life is there in everybody, but there are few and far between who wish to struggle for it to help others. We are, of course, confident that when call comes from those who are sincere and well meaning people's response would be there. They have a long history which confirms that from time to time new values and tradition were implanted in their minds. Old structures of thought were updated and revised from time to time. Resistance to change in many does not continue for long. Human life has to concede change since it cannot be governed by an intellectually formulated doctrine drawn up for all times. It is always in movement.

A Serious Problem

It may be pointed out that in our times most of our talented young men and women do not opt for dabbling in politics or for undertaking some social work as a matter of profession. They are security oriented. They prefer to undertake some petty but remunerative jobs in which they aspire to out do their friends and colleagues. Political fields are left open to others. As a result, cetrain unscrupulous elements have captured the way and occupy important social and political positions. Some of them have even reached very high. There are records how a few have climbed up unopposed. As a result, the entire society is lying at their feet. This is the actual political and social arrangement under which we happen to live. This is our exact system. Other things are stated in the books for our young students to study and forget them as they grow up and enter the struggle for life.

Time

The order of time is very important. The individual is physically destined to live in the present though he works for the future. He can, of course, transport himself in the domains of past as well as in future through aids of memory or imagination, but not in actuality. The past is available in the form of memory. He makes use of it in shaping the present. He visualises future on the basis of his past and present experiences.

There is a strange tendency amongst certain people that they prefer to live mentally in the past. They feel safe in that world. The present is extremely disheartening to them. They believe that their lives should have been designed on the patterns laid down by their ancestors.

Such people are dragged by the forces of history. They fail to grasp the spirit of their own times since the past is heavily controlling their psyches. They remain ill equipped to face present and future effectively as their entire thinking and preparation of life is revolving around the past. It is the solemn duty of each and every individual to live and operate in his own times and draw the blue prints of future.

As soon as future is concretised, it would become present and gradually a matter of the past. Time is not a commodity.

School clildren solve the questions of "time and work". Here its costing is worked out. On the other hand life-time is a different phenomenon. It is not sold in the market. So it is very precious. It should not be wasted. Once it has passed, it cannot be recalled.

This awareness is very important in the life of an individual "Now or Never."

Era

The conquest of material side of individual's life had all along been considered as something of lesser consequence in Indian thought. Of late, living conditions have been fast changing and the time old thought is being scrutinised. Till fifties an average educated Indian had not forgotten the advice of late Sir Syed Ahmed Khan and Swami Vivekananda and many others that he should have strictly adhered on to his spiritual traditions. This holds good in the countryside even today. "Purely physical dominance is mechanical" said Tagore, "and modern machines are merely exaggerating our bodies lengthening and multiplying our limbs. The modern mind, in its innate childishness, delights in this enormous bodily bulk, representing inordinate material power, saying, let me have the big toy and no sentiment which can disturb it"

Now times are changed. That was an era when India and Indian spirit were to be saved from the attacks of westernisation. Many of our leaders who upheld the cause of new thinking were not distinguishing between "modernisation" and "westernisation." Tagore was no exception. In our times, technological progress has reached too far. We are feeling its impact in our normal living. It is no longer the prerogative of the West. Other peoples of the world including those of India are making mark in various fields of science and technology. The over all performance of Indian scientists both in India and abroad is commendable. Industrial Revolution has been picking up all over the world. The influences of science and technology are affecting the social fabric and that are bound to generate new conditions from where new implications for social and political life would emerge.

Fundamentalism

The fundamentalists would try to build up something impossible on the dilapidated walls of the past cultures and religions. They would not be able to achieve much since the spirit of our age is driving the forces of history in a different direction. There is frantic search for objectivity and rationality for human activities in the institutes of higher learning.

In the scientific thought of the twentieth century there is an accepted element of "probability". So far social science is concerned, its possibility is taken for granted. Formulas bequeathed by the medieval ages are not considered workable. People can be momentarily excited to achieve something spectacular in the names of beliefs but it would be soon realised by those who are in the fray that they were misguided. Men are capable of both great altruism as well as of venality. Efforts are to be made that they should exorcise the latter. They are to be persuaded for campassion against indifference. Our basic objective should be to stand for some illuminating humanism. Once it is clearly understood many positive human values would begin to attract people.

Struggles

With the all round increase of production of those material articles that we need, human desire for acquiring them more has also increased. At the same time who would like to imperil those benefits which have already been realised. The people's standard of living has been fast improving, they look for more comforts and security and over it less hard work. In the given circumstances, only those would be attracted by the struggles who are living in dire poverty. Only they would fight for seizing certain benefits. As soon as these are made available to them, the intensity of their will to fight for is bound to enervate. Solzhenitsyn, the noted Soviet novelist and the Nobel Laureate, has stated that where "Such a decline in courage is particularly noticeable among the ruling and intellectual elite, causing an impression of a loss of courage by the entire society".

Advice

Here is a point of consideration for the common folk who have some understanding of things to pluck the courage and align themselves with those forces that are trying to resolve the issues which confront the entire human race. What is against mankind, would not be helpful to Indians or Chinese or Pakistanis, or Americans or Soviets.

A few simple goals can therefore be proposed. It is alright to make bold statements in seminars and in debates but it is extremely difficult to contact people and then suggest such programmes which are not likely to yield immediate benefits. We do not expect much from those channels of communication that are managed by the State. They abide by the instructions issued by the rulers. They ary least concerned with the larger objectives of man and mankind. So it is proposed that the traditional means of contacting the people should be activated. The generation of new sense of commitment amongst the people is an important work. We cannot raise new temples simply from the debris of old ones. For that new data and material are also to be collected and then fresh foundations of new ideals laid. We can anticipate, there would be lot of opposition to all positive moves, but that is inevitable. If rulers fail, leaders avoid, and the elite do not rise to the occasion then who would meet the situation ? The proposed new task forces should become the vanguard for creating new times. We should not permit the conditions to drift.

Real Task

Although the study of this march of entire human race is not that simple, still it is to be deliberated by many subtle minds of our times. Solutions may come in sight just by drawing blue prints of a few plans or programmes, but the task of their execution would remain. Indian mind has length, breadth and even depth all at once and is, of course, quite adept in visualising things beyond horizon. Some thing happens to it during implementation of the projects. Here is our collapse. We get incapacitated by our own mental make up. For that, certain new attitudes are to be cultivated amongst the people so that they may courageously confront the emerging present and the developing future. They should not stop just at discussing the ins and outs of the issues rather plunge in the considered action for doing the needful. They should feel that they are fighting out their own battle. They are not mercenaries. Their own interests are directly involved. The benefits would ultimately flow to them.

Individual

"If we are self centred and think merelyin terms of our own interests, we have no moral right to blame state or society for playing foul with us. Instead of expecting much from others we should ask ourselves as what we are doing for ourselves, as well as for others. It goes without saying that certain material comforts are necessary for a modcrate living, but the individual should not remain all absorbed in producing and enjoying them. He must devote some of his time and energy to the simple thought as to how he can make this world better than he has found it. He has to think and work for earning good bread, seeking a fine life partner, producing bright children, living in a well built houses and so on, but a stage should come in his life when his mind should transcend such common ambitions. In other words, he should arm his self with certain higher objectives of life. He must grow and enrich his potentialities. He must acknowledge the rights of others to grow and prosper. He must build up his courage and express his views fearlessly. He should have an inquiring and experimenting mind. He may err. He may have the veracity to acknowledge it. He is to remain hopeful even under the most trying circumstances. Over it, he might ponder over future of mankind and contemplate regarding the mysteries of life. According to F. Dostoyeysky, the famous Russian novelist of the last century, "Man is a mystery that must be solved, and if you spend your entire life in solving it, do not say that you have wasted your time."

New Man

For extrinsic life, i.e. for living in the society, man has to be action oriented. For intrinsic development' he is to plumb deeper depths of his mind. Efforts on both sides are to be made simultaneously and their meeting stations set up so that the process of their interaction is eased. A disconnected state of see-saw in theory and practice would lead to nothingness in the life of man. Suitable steps are to be taken so that a situation of the kind does not arise. If there is sun outside, there are eyes inside. If there is knowledge outside, there is wisdom inside. If there is air outside, there are lungs inside. If there is food outside, there is stomach inside. If there is challenge outside, there is will inside. So man is like that of a coin. He has two sides, but coin is one. Man is one. If we wish that individual should do his best, inside him he should be thoughtful, masterful and resolute and not nervous, or coward or even quick tempered. "Every life", Aurobindo said, "is a step which can take backward or forward by his action, his will in life, by the thought and knowledge that governs it, he determines what he is yet to be". A common man saves himself from the possibilities of debilitation if he enriches his world of thought, but it is not enough that he has integrated himself with some higher cause, his activities should also demonstrate this position.

13

LEADERSHIP (PART I)

"Historical events, and the role of historical personalities, teach us mainly, if not perhaps primarily, how not to act. Acting & creation cannot be taught literally. To say this does not diminish the significance of historical events and personalities ; none of it will diminish Tito, or the events in which he played so decisive a role. Life and politics are irrepressible, ever new, recreated, only if they exert the will to resist not and not fall into decay."

Milovan Djilas

"Life is like a game of bridge. We did not invent the game or design thc cards. We did not frame the rules and we cannot control the dealing Cards are dealt to us whether they be good or bad. To that extent determinism rules. But we can play the game well or play it boldly. A skilful player may have a poor hand and yet win the game. A bad player may have a good hand and yet mak ; a mess of it. Our life is a mixture of necessity and freedom, chance and choice. By exercising our choice properly we can control steadily all elements and eliminate altogether the determinism of nature."

Dr. S. Radhakrishnan

Leadership as a phenomenon has been noticed amongst different species of animals. It is not only men and women who choose or elect or select or just get some leaders. A leader is supposed to play a notable role in shaping the people's destiny. So far his physical side is concerned, he appears to be a man of common size. Still others look towards him for help and security just as children do in respect of their father. People believe that leader is capable of safeguarding them from all calamities. They quote from his past performances. He has weathered through many stormy events that shook the foundations of the well entrenched forces and he is considered fit to take charge of the situation.

His efforts may end in fiasco or he may come to power. Whatever may be the consequences, he is required to demonstrate that he is not wreckless. He has no dark side of life. It is either suppressed or thoroughly masked. He would live and die for some higher cause. People are dear to him. If he has been thrown up by some revolution or say by some great movement, he obviously qualifies many tests since he has passed through many difficult situations with courage and distinction otherwise he would have been swept away by the storms of history. People watch when he operates from high positions for some time and his performance proves his capacities beyond all doubts.

If he has come to power through some manipulation or say by the support of the army by some other short cut, he is always rated as an average leader till he proves otherwise while being in some highest office. But if he has been voted to power by the people, he has a long way to go in convincing them that he possesses all merit to occupy high position. The victory is achieved through ballot and thereafter he is placed at the top. Here is an opportunity in which he can demonstrate his real potential. History confirms that many mediocrities had achieved celebrated political positions but they were no leaders of consequence.

Movement

When a revolutionary movement picks up, there are many who enter the race. Some of them have lofty ambitions to realise. Out of them quite a few are eliminated or killed in the long drawn struggles that are opened. Even if they disappear from the scene, their impact is felt. Their services are acknowledged. People recall their sacrifices. A few others are knocked out since they fail to go far with the movement as it does not unfold itself in accordance with the original promise which had fascinated them. Some may even get unnerved while confronting heavy odds. There are still a few more who go confused and in the process their perceptions get blurred under trying circumstances and thus they lose the focus. There is of course a negligible number of those who correctly read what is written on the wall of future.

The people come to salute them since they are the rising suns. Men like Lenin, Gandhi, Mao, Tito and Ho Chi Minh are those who led the revolutions and movements in our times and have gone down in the human history as great leaders in the real sense of the term. Well, they were Men amongst men, not just tricky wickets".

Not a Messiah

A leader is a leader. He is not a prophet or a messiah. He is not a man riding on a horse and as if all others are walking as a crowd. He is not to sit in a balcony for receiving salutations of his people. He is to face rivals both from amongst his friends as well as foes. A good number of people may be with him but others are also there not well disposed towards him. There were other leaders with people too when Lenin, Gandhi, Mao and others were engaged in their struggles. Times move on and they had been successful. Their opponents are forgotten. All opposition fades away gradually. It may have committed certain follies or not but is not in a position to hold on. Gradually a leader acquires an unrivalled position. People now put all trust in him. His image is magnified. There is a proverb in Persian that saints do not fly, their followers remember them to have done so. They treat him as an angel. The dwindling opponents may gnash their teeth as and when he is referred. What more can they do ?

Once he is at the helm of the affairs, he has to be very tactful. His each and every move is to be calculated. He also takes suitable steps for the liquidation of those who would not permit him to deliver goods but all this is achieved quietly.

Leader's Approach

First of all, he should throw up such programmes that may appeal directly to the largest number of people. He should prove it beyond all doubt that his commitment to the welfare of the poor and downtrodden amongst them is total. In a country like India more production of goods, their fair distribution, no wastage of resources and no exploitation of the people at the grass root level are the major objectives for realisation.

He should concentrate all his energies in ensuring that his programmes are set in achieving these ends and he would make all possible efforts to achieve them in a time frame. Targets should be achievable. He should so behave, as if he is not against his opponents, i.e. "malice towards none". He may even approach them for seeking their support. He should play his cards so astutely that his strength is proved. He is no superman but he is all conscious of his responsibilities. He must have better political instinct than others. Ideas may strike to him before others could think of them. In that case opponents would not be able to cut much ice. "Opposition" for the sake of "opposition" is no programme to which people would support for long. This is a negative approach and they understand it. A leader need not unnecessarily condemn the stalwarts of opposition by mentioning their names. He should rather discuss their programmes and policies and pinpoint their futility. As far as possible he should avoid frontal attacks. It is a chaotic age, we are on the threshold of many revolutions. A leader shall have to go into the heart of things and help in shaping events in such a manner that his aspirations are realised at the earliest.

He lives in his own times and visualises what is possible in the foreseeable future. His imagination and creative powers should always aim at achieving something consequential. Petty gains of personal life should not come in his way. If he has not been able to address himself to this issue, he may quietly walk out of arena. A leader would fail his family. He is no longer a domestic bird. He is found neglecting his parents, wife and children. Their neglect is quoted as a proof of his selflessness.

He may get data collected through others, but he must interpret it himself and innovate such ideas which are pregnant with future possibilities. He may so express them that people would be benefited by their implementation. In this way, he builds up the confidence of common people. They have otherwise no faith in themselves. Now they discover that they are capable of doing things better.

Whatever may be the hardships, he should never entertain pessimism or fatalism to over take his mind. He is a fountain of hope since it is always in love with success. This would help him to collect his powers even after defeats. That also confirms that he is grappling with the issues with courage and ability. He is all involved in their being thrashed out. He is against the approach of a pigeon who closes its eyes at the sight of a wily cat, since that would not save the life of the said bird.

He-man

Leader is a He-man. He would fight and fight to the bitter end. If the nerve breaking experiences do not frustrate him, he would acquire maturity of very high level one day. This is a positive development of his personality and it would place him much ahead of his rivals. Victories should make him humane, sober and saner, but it does not always happen. Element of pride gets somewhere injected in his head. It is to be weeded out. For achieving this he may transfer all credit to his friends and followers whose cooperation had led to his success.

The defeats should be faced with patience. He should critically examine as to why he could not anticipate them. There is very thin line that divides success and failure. A particular set of conditions is always pervailing. The same methodology could have resulted in any possibility. Life is a strange coin and its two sides have opposite inscriptions. Success on one side and defeat on the other. Strategies might be revised in view of new experiences, but he should not easily give way on the issue of causes he is championing. Collapse of a leader may not be the failure of a cause or an ideology.

Defeats

In the grave battles of life many events would come and go and where ups and downs are inevitable, but a right commander would remain composed and unperturbed. He must live and act gracefully under all circumstances. It is easier to write so in a booklet, but the wearer knows where and how the shoe pinches. Still there is no other positive advice which could have been suggested to an aspirant. Certain defeats are of course terrible in their after effects. A leader may be thrown to a wall. Even then he should not abandon his efforts. He has an effective tongue. His pen his powerful. His eyes are sharp. He should make full use of his expression. It must stand for confidence courage, and strong sense of sacrifice for the values he has been fighting for. He should always bear in mind that people are watching him. Even if, he is not in power, he is being shadowed by friends and foes. In the Indian situation he has to qualify as "super man" prescribed by Aurobindo or Iqbal.

Action

So right course for a leader is to remain always in ferment. He must take it that time at his disposal is very short and the work that is to be completed by him is enormous. Each and every minute matters and so it should be rightly and fully utilised. It would never return in his life time. He should therefore always be involved in the affairs both emotionally and intellectually.

If his conscience is clear and he has no personal axe to grind, his mind and body would feel all liberated and elevated from all hardships that life generates in its onward march. This attitude goes too far in shaping the course of his life. It would slow down the process of his ageing. If there are conflicts in his mind and he is not following the course dictated by his better self, he would feel all miserable and start decaying quickly. He should never allow his rivals to outsmart him in discharging his functions. He should so organise his daily routine of life that he does not stop growing in information, knowledge and in discharging his duties that he has imposed on himself. Leadership is not a part time or a casual profession.

During the preparatory period of his life he should have studied the biographies and autobiographies of the great leaders. They had their own sets of problems and conditions. They had grappled with the issues and at times more serious issues than of his own times. Here his perceptive mind should work. He has his own problems. His conditions are there. His information about the world around is there. He picks up the situation.

It would be just like throwing a stone in the lake of his mind. He is in motion. His memory, motivation, knowledge, ideology, expectations, ambitions, distractions and even health are interacting. He must study even the epics and other classics which form the heritage of his society as well as of the peoples of the world. Their influences on the minds of all are deeply etched. Different sides of life which he is leading should be critically examined and discussed with all scholars or friends. How can he be dynamic and original in his approach until and unless he is aware of all undercurrents and secret developments that are taking place around him ? Society is not an aeroplane where a pilot is required to press the buttons and pull the levers. It is not a well maintained machine. A great leader is required to be an inspirational force. He is not a manager or a bureaucrat. People place their trust in him. If he succeeds in achieving something, his stature is magnified. Admirers and followers all hail him an incarnation, a messiah, a prophet and what not. His victories may be defeats of others within or without the society. The adversely affected people would denounce him as a demon, a Satan, a villain and so on. Well, it is clearly conceded by all that he matters. He is a force.

Down to the Earth

A leader is to remain down to the earth. He needs not build up castles in the air. His ideology is the base over which he stands and explains to the people as to how the forces of history are at work and what should be done in the existing state of affairs. For him 'ideology' is not a bundle of formulas which are to be used, rather he means that suitable suggestions being thrown up by it should be plucked and examined through further debates and discussions as to how these could be applied sagaciously. Blind followers lead to disasters. Suitable modifications in the ideologies are to be made from time to time in view of changing conditions. These are not horoscopes.

Ideological interpretations would certainly provide credibility to his pronouncements but he should not so tie himself with them as if he has nothing more to say or do. Times are changing. Conditions are changing too. Circumstances are changing. Situations are changing. With all that needs are changing.

Leader has his ideology, plans, and purposes. He has passionate concern with his objectives. At the same time he is the centre of responsibilities. He is to interact with the issues around and achieve what is best possible. Ideology convinces his followers to a considerable degree that he is not going astray. They are more committed to ideology than to a leader. His substitute is round the corner and that is not so in the case of ideology.

14

LEADERSHIP (PART II)

"The concept of leadership should be understood as encompassing a wide range of activities. It applies to the running of small groups and the governing of nations. It may concern the relatively diffuse process of influence in establishing norms of style or opinion or it may involve specific orders in a chain of command. It includes supervision and statesmanship, routine administration and organisation building. Interpretations of leadership as a sociological concept have changed over the years. The total effort of sociologists can be seen as an attempt to develop conceptions that apply to a variety of social systems including those that prevailed in the past as well as those now emerging. The need for more general conceptions is also felt as a need to understanding leadership within the widely differeing social and political contexts that exist in the modern world."

Arnold S. Tannenbaum

The leader is made of the same clay as a common man is madeof.Still the former has more of innate strength. His political and social instincts are stronger than others. He has more of courage and ability. Common man possesses certain principles, but he may not like to sacrifice for them, but that is not the case with a leader. He would patiently pass through all the circumstances, however difficult these might be. He would assure the people that he would do and die for them. That would provide psychological security to them. It is a normal attitude of a common man to seek "compensations for personal limitations." He shirks his responsibilities and therefore cannot help depending on a leader.

A leader must have the instinctive capacity of adjusting, or compromising with the conditions but without deflecting from the goal that he has set for himself as well as for his followers. If some new ideas have struck to him he should very carefully point them out. These are to be presented as the logical extension of the ideology to which he is committed. People would then believe that he is not deviating from the path already laid before them. They are undoubtedly self-seekers but they would never accept a leader being so. He should always be found swimming in the high tides of selflessness.

Sobriety

When the tempers of the people are very high and they are out for some kind of showdown, or for violence, he should demonstrate his patience courage and sobriety. For that, he should not run away from the scene. It is the prerogative of common people to unleash their irrational impulses and put everything in disarray. A leader shall have to proceed other way round. He should be very dexterous in handling all the issues especially those in which sentiments and beliefs of the people are involved. They are very touchy in these areas of their lives.

There are moments in history when some of their riligious traditions are put to severe scrutiny. It is perhaps easier to surcharge the minds of the people with the ideas of wars and revolution, but to prepare them to accept changes on sensitive religious, moral and social values is a very difficult task. They would quote history of going to the gallows for adhering to their position instead of submitting to the proposed changes. They nostalgically love certain things and refuse to get out of their influences. Leader shall have to be tactful and courageous fight out his way over his followers. It is not a simple affair. His position may be imperilled. Still he has to bear in mind that existing world order is to be improved. He knows it well. It is to be changed. Emerging situations are to be anticipated and what is possible in the over all interests of the people is to be focussed and efforts are to be made for realising the same. This is though inherent in the situation and for that he has to proceed dialectically. Many sincere, honest and well meaning leaders collapse at times since they fail to plan their activities under the conditions which are pregnant with unusual and hazy possibilities. Dicisions are note made in the vacuum. A leader cannot depend upon visualising abstractions. He has to interact with hard but actual realities of his own times.

Strategy

There are obstacles in his path that he should confront and try to remove the same in such a manner that unnecessary opposition is not generated. Here lies the test of his courage and ability. Application of suitable strategy at crucial moments is absolutely necessary. He should quietly pierce through the events and avoid to seek his way through "blowing trumpets". Let the people debate afterward, as to how he has conducted and created the history. If he is quiet and avoids self-praise, it would strike as if he is lying low though in the heart of his hearts he is clear that he is leading the events according to his plans.

He may at times permit certain incidents to take place and wait at some flagstations of life to watch the events but there should be no compromise on essentials. He is to be all clear about his objectives. Adroit followers or clever opponents might discover the threads of his strategy but he himself should remain reticent. Handling of intricate problems that confront a society is not simple affair. In the words of Mr. Rajiv Gandhi, "There is so much free play in the controls that you can at the most shake them at one end and nothing happens at the other—inertia is great." It takes best out of a man and still it is not sure he would succeed. He is involved in a great effort. There is no book containing the complete blue prints of correct actions. No individual has ever been born to be omniscient.

Clarity

A leader may be clear as to what he is doing but people would come to the end of tunnel after certain events have taken place and the struggle for proposed objectives reaches some crucial stage and history has unfolded itself in a big way. Leader faces a severe test then. If he has integrity, up-righteousness and loyalty to the people, and he is trying to achieve what is possible with the resources at his command, he may meet success. Failure is not ruled out. Even if he is defeated after he has boldly and rightly acted and reacted in the entire struggle, some of the people would acknowledge his merit. In our recent history we have an illustrious example of Late Shri Jaya Prakash Narayan who always stood for justice, truth and righteousness. He never submitted to authority abandoning these priciples. He stood all firm so far his principles were concerned. Over it he had no love for power. He was also an apostle of peace. Finally he also noticed the smiles of history before paying his debt to nature.

Failure

Well, who does not fail ? Who is never defeated ? Perhaps None. Failures are the stepping stones to success. We can guess. We can hope. We can wish. We can aspire. We can predict. We can do many things but we can not guarantee success even after all calculations and taking righteous actions. Success cannot be predicted till it has been achieved and in our harsh world nothing succeeds like success. We can fight against our failings but not against all the failures, except through trying again.

Changing Perceptions

The leader is, at times, charged of even treachary if he tries to revise his positions. There are many hard nuts in the society who are not in a position to reflect, but they are very vociferous in criticism. A lot of caution is therefore required on the part of a leader. He is operating in a fast changing world. Here every thing is in flux. Now if he changes his position on a particular issue, he is required to prove it that he has no personal axe to grind and in the circumstances he cannot afford to adhere to those positions that were proposed some time back. The silencing of irresponsible criticism at such critical moments requires lot of skill and statesmanship. Since he is in the think of fiery struggles his perceptions are bound to change, but he has to take his people with him.

We see many self proclaiming leaders who have no following. They speak, write and go to the people but receive no response. If masses are not there to follow a leader, he is reduced to the position of a petty teacher or a worker or say a writer of no consequence.

Masses are like the leaves of a tree. Branches are like those of the activists of the social and political life of a society. Programmes are the trunk. Ideology is at the roots. The spirit of the whole tree is exposed by the leaders. They should be able to demonstrate the results if all parts of the body of the tree have life.

Learning

There is an erroneous belief that a leader must be a man of great learning. He is not to be a book worm. Men like, Gandhi, Tagore, Aurobindo, Nehru, Azad and many others had been scholars and men of great learning. They were at the same time representing very high culture of the land. Most of them had entered politics under the promptings of their conscience. Had the country been not languishing under the heels of the British imperialism, they would have stuck to their respective fields of specialisation. Their illustrious example has bequeathed a view that our leadership should not be exclusively political. Their interests in other areas of life are also important. Scholarship may be an important quality of a leader but it is not enough. He has to be a past master of the political affairs, since these are concentrated form of activities through which societies are built up.

Wisdom

We can collect data. We can borrow information. We can learn from books. We can gain experience but all said and done, we can not have wisdom like this. Montaingue had very precisely stated : "It was a paradoxical command that was given us of old by that god at Delphi," Look into yourself, know yourself, keep to yourself ; bring back your mind and your will, which are spending themselves elsewhere, into themselves, you are running out, you are scattering yourself, concentrate yourself, resist yourself, you are being betrayed, dispersed and stolen away from yourself. Do you not see that this would keeps its sight all concentrated inward, and its eyes open to contemplate itself ? It is always vanity for you, within and without ; but it is less vanity when it is less extensive except for you. Oman said that god each thing studies itself first and according to its needs has limits to its labours and desires. There is not a single thing as empty and needy, as you, who embrace the universe ; you are the investigator without knowledge, the magistrate without jurisdiction and all in all, the food of the farce''. Wisdom is something inside. It is like that of a fountain. It would bubble out as we dig it. The more we dig inside, it grows outside. Whatever may be the position of a leader, the possibilities of his further digging in himself do not exhaust.

Each leader is to be himself. He can borrow statements from Marx or Gandhi or Mao, but that would not make him a leader. ''Everyone has the obligation'', said Cicero, to ponder will his own specific traits of character. He must also regulate them adequately and not wonder whether some one else's traits might suit him better. The more definitely his own a man's character is the better it fits him''. His deeper self has memory, impact of past experiences, knowledge, perceptions and so on. From outside he must be a man of broad and profound knowledge and understanding regarding history, politics, economics society, religion, culture, modern science technology and so on. By temperament he should be scientific in his approach and a dynamic personality. A leader relies more on his own potentials. His capacities are enormous. He can reach unprecedented heights and help out his friends, relatives, society, state and so on. For acheving all this he has to get out of the routinised lives of his contemporary leaders.

Scholar vs. Leader

A leader is generally a different human material from that of a scholar. It is said that there are many who fail in the turmoils and quietly migrate to teaching and writing or to some professions where they can demonstrate their learning and a bit of experience. A scholar is a reservoir of information, whereas a leader is objective, clear, bold, and above all very intelligent. Even common man with average ability wishes to lead his life well. If he climbs a bit, he would try to understand its ins and outs, its beauty, and ugliness, its greatness and meanness and so on. If he ascends slightly more he would improve it for others to the extent possible. If he goes up like a rocket, he would transform its character for millions and millions. A leader's profession demands that he should align himself with some higher cause perdict about those possibilities that are achievable with the efforts proposed, he tries to take charge of the situation and pushes the peoples to the desired ends. He then becomes an important instrument in shaping tomorrow. Well, his efforts may not drive the historic forces exactly in the pointed direction proposed by him, still his influences can be perceived. A scholar would be collecting details and provide insight as to how the minds of others are working. He is capable of conceiving, foreseeing, knowing the misfortunes of others, but he fail to discover his own understanding and knowledge through which he could have turned the pages of history

Followers

A leader tries to find his "self" in the selves of all and locates all other selves in his own self. In other words he identifies himself with the important interests of others. He is a drop, a glistening drop in the ocean of the society. His greatness lies in handling the critical situations with dignity, poise and firmness. He should be in a position to convince others that he matters and thus be treated seriously. He should be in control of the situations and valiantly resist the drift which sets the people for decay. Many enervating forces are always at work. Some of them even do not come to lime light and great damage is caused. If the leader has the grip over the circumstances he would weed them out.

Times

Times have become more complicated. In the past as aspiring leader in India was required to be a man of good physique, robust in his articulation, adept in organising meetings, processions, fluttering of banners and so on, but many of these qualities have become irrelevant in our times. E ven hunger strikes and jail going exercises do not impress upon the people since the latter ridicule such gimmicks. Imperialism and colonialism are no longer the issues that should rivet the attention of the leadership. Different problems are now there. People ask straight questions. What is leadership doing for removing hunger ? What steps are being taken for generating employment? Why are these appalling differences between productivity and production ? Who are responsible for this nonsense ? What actions are being taken against those who are exploiting the poor masses ? What are the hopes for millions and millions ? How would they actualise them ?

Survival of a leader

A leader should have certain heroic qualities but he is not just a hero. We meet many young people who are very ambitious and wish to do some thing spectacular. They may succeed and thereafter continue in the social and political life. If they survive for a reasonable period they may become leaders. This is a strange and cruel world. Many well meaning and honest leaders had been crushed by unscrupulous elements.

On the other hand, there are some dare devils who emerge on the firmament and hold the scene but for a short while. They have a cause to fight for but fail to appreciate the far reaching implications of the issues which are in the womb of the social conditions. Their style is generally wreckless but at the same time they are pure and clean. We note a flash in their personalities. They are generally killed or hanged. Their charisma is of short duration. All out efforts are made by certain forces to oust them from the arena, but their dramatic performances are liked by the people in general. Their influence in history is acknowledged since they make and unmake events to a certain degree.

As compared to them, a great leader traverses a long period of trials and tribulations. He understands the issues with more clarity. He grasps the spirit of the age through the windows of history, culture, economics, philosophy, religion, science, psychology, sociology, anthropology etc. We should not forget that an aged leader can preserve his youthful spirits if he so wishes. Spirit has no biological age. He acquires some sort of magnetism in his personality through sufferings and sacrificing for others. Austerity is an other important quality of a leader. It has a great appeal in our country. He is not a dare devil but he has immense courage and ability to meet the challenges. Age turns him chastened and quiet but this is not his indifference. His maturity is based on his long and arduous experience. "Old places and old powers," remarked George Santayana, "in their turn when spirit dwells in them have an intrinsic vitality of which youth is incapable precisely the balance and wisdom that come from long perspectives and broad foundations".

15

MOVEMENT (PART I)

"Extraordinary times demand extraordinary action."

Ludwig Beck

"We should go into the midst of the masses, learn from them, sum up their experiences so that these experiences will become well defined principles and methods, and then explain them to the masses (through agitation work) and call upon the masses to put them into practice in order to solve their problems and lead them to liberation of happiness"

Mao Tse Tung

Movements confirm that a particular society is in ferment i.e. its people are aspiring to organise themselves for achieving certain higher objectives. They are not a dead mass. They are watching the changing spectrum. They are aware of their problems. They might plan to grapple with them. They are not taking things for granted. They are ready for getting mobilised at the first opportunity.

Ours is a very large society in which millions and millions of people are involved. Everybody matters. He or she is important and matters at his or her place. If there is no epochal movement to push them all towards some goal, they are likely to waste their energies for seizing petty personal gains and get crippled in the historical sense of the term.

We are a multi-cultural and even multi-civilisational society. People have varied styles of living. All cannot be put together.

Their pursuits are not identical. Their ambitions are not similar. Their religious beliefs vary. They do not abide by particular sets of social norms. Their faiths also do not drive them to one end. Still the fact remains that they are destined to live and work together. They have no other alternative. What they badly need is a strong sense of humaneness and reasonableness. They are to safeguard and expand the web of their freedom as well as help others to do so. They should feel passionately concerned with the well-being of one another. They have to get out of themselves and align with something higher.

Those who believe themselves to be activists, are to plan a programme that should appeal and assure the people that it would help them all to progress in the details of their material and other levels of living. Benefits would flow to them in direct proportion to the length, breadth and depth of their efforts. Immediate beginnings to this effect may be made. Assurances may be given that the exploiters would be kept out so that the fruits of people's labour should reach them even at the bottom level. If a movement is organised on these simple and straightforward principles, that would help the people in discovering their own possibilities. We have specific conditions. Real progress is possible if changes take place in economic, socio-political and cultural spheres of their lives. If some advancement is registered in one direction and other sides are left unattended, that would lead to disaster.

Direction

It is very important that we should not be just a rudderless lot of people. There is no place for high sounding ambitions in our calculations. We are to be poised for doing what is possible. Broader objectives are to be clear and then try to build up a movement which may help us in realising what is the best in the given conditions. As soon as some of the programmes have been implemented, new horizons may emerge and even then there would be no let up in our efforts. Our society as we see it to-day is not a blank piece of papers. It is five thousand years old. We are not entirely of our own creation. We have been made and marred by historic influences. Time is ripe that we should fix up a few new goals to achieve as otherwise we may go down in the history as a "wasted generation". The possibilities for improving the existing arrangements are always to be searched. This is a dialectical process.

Fresh social, economic, political cultural, sociological and psychological studies regarding our people, are to be made. Their unexpressed ideas and ambitions are to be discovered. India is an open society and here each and every individual who is alive matters. He is not a mutton. He is required to play his role with gusto and enthusiasm. Well, we are addressing him to join certain future streams of struggles where he should demonstrate his best. Movement is a very big chain and here he is supposed to be its important ring. If he breaks the entire chain would fail. The movement would go to the dogs. He therefore holds a crucial position.

Individual

Society and state may not accord him the dignity he deserves. He should not of course be treated casually. On the other hand, he has certain responsibilities. He is not just a biological or a sociological entity. He is required to transcend. He should behave like a full man. From distance, he may strike to be a simple, an illiterate and all worthless. That is not so. He has certain possibilities which are to be discovered and then strengthened for his full development. If he progresses, he helps the entire society to look up. The best technique of persuading him is to adopt face to face communication method. Its impact is very profound. He may ask questions, at times intricate questions, personal questions which have concern with his social life. All these are to be replied befittingly. A common man would not bend easily. He would stick to his positions. He would argue, discuss and debate and offer strong resistence. The members of the "Task forces" who have to persuade him are to be torch bearers and educators. They must satisfy him if he is to do his best.

This right to vote just after every five years cannot inspire him to do or die for a leader or a party or society. He is to be inspired for searching a lofty cause to which he should align and lead his life. He must get such conditions in which he may display his ability, courage and determination. Whatever constructive is sown in his mind, it would bear fruit. If he comes to know the improved methods of agriculture, namely in tillage, planting, use of fertilisers and good seeds, treatment of plants, drainage system, new harvesting technology, he wouid respond provided he is assured that benefits would flow to him.

Planners should not always remind him to make sacrifices. He must feel convinced that he is not being exploited and he is getting due of his past performances. Life between the individual and the state or thc society is not to be organised as a one way traffic. He is generally found complainıng that he has been doing his best and has suffered a lot over a considerable period. After all there is a limit to which he could have stretched himself. Long spells of sufferings and sacrifices have demoralised him. Now if he really reaps a few benefits, that would kindle hope and some thrill in his day to day life.

Who would like to work for the selfish leaders or for a diseased party ? Even party workers of our times ask strange questions about their leader. They cannot get out of this mental conditions. On the other hand people expect higher level of ethics from them at least. If the party activists are worthless, they would fail in inspiring people. Motivating people for launching major movements is a gigantic task, but once people's imagination is rightly fired, they would turn the page of history. Leadership should however ensure that these effort, are essentially an informal education of the people. They are to be enlightened for restructuring their lives. Here entire population, irrespective of caste, creed, religion, place of domicile, is to be involved. Times are gone when people could be so mobilised for war efforts. Here is an offensive for peace and prosperity. We do not mean to build up the power of the rulers but of the people. They should think and look up. The new arrangements should reflect that it is people's movement.

New Age

At the moment we are on the threshold of a new age. A nation wide movement is required to help people for rebuilding their social, economic, political, cultural, and spiritual spheres of their lives. Say, if we try to float an organisation for building up Dharamshalas, Gurdwaras and Mosques, that would not tone up the religious thoughts of the people. There are already so many religious places lying unattended and mismanaged. Priority may be given to put them in order instead of raising new ones for neglect and decay.

The similar argument can be advanced if decision is taken for attending to some other traditional activity. There is an urgent need of such organisations that should inspire our people to look forward. Let us strengthen our efforts for increasing jobs both for the skilled and unskilled. Let us increase the facilities of informal education in the rural side of the country. Let us disseminate technical and ideological knowledge. The impulse of doing something plausible has always been there amongst the people, but social, political and cultural hinderances are there.

Culture in a particular age is composed of so many traits that people have in their personalities. Here it is also important to record that these are always changing. Fresh studies should be made regarding our attitudes towards law and order, state, society, leadership, women liberation, agriculture, industries, urbanisation, poverty, manual work, religion, spiritualism and so on. Since existing order of things is crumbling, new ideas and practices are to be introduced. What exactly should be done may perhaps be found in books and journals, but what is possible to achieve in the given conditions and can be had is only through a movement. Best possible minds that are available with us are to be deployed. So many options are to be considered, priorities are to be worked out and people are to be convinced that right direction has been found. Here it would not be out of place to state that scrapping of certain old irrelevant values or attitudes is a difficult task. We condemn many evils on objective and rational scales on paper as well as in meetings but otherwise they remain in occupation of our minds. For example, we denounce dowry system, but it is practised. There was a movement Indian National Congress prior to the year 1947. Hereafter it was reduced to a political party in power. It is now ailing.

Industrial Society

We are in the process of raising a very large industrial society with some kind of tilt towards our Indianness. Our past, present and future are in severe conflicts, over here. Industrialisation comes out of the womb of science and technology and for it we need a social organisation that upholds to generate scientific temper amongst his people. The prevailing social order seeks strength from agricultural life. In view of new social and economic needs, new demands are being raised and these come in conflict with the existing order. That is why we find so many tensions around. Increased sense of alienation is there. The community feeling in general is no longer visible. The harmonious relationships are debated as a matter of the past.

It can be understood that we cannot exactly estimate the total possible product in agriculture. We may sow two Mango seeds of the same variety in one orchard. These may be looked after by the same gardener. The same quantity and quality of fertilisers and water may be made available to the seedlings to become plants and then trees. But still we cannot say that their produce of man goes would be be equal. The same is true for the most of harvests of our world. The same may be true for all animals including those of human beings in respect of their potential but so far industry is concerned, such vagaries are very very limited.

Industrial Growth

Industrial growth can be broadly conceived, planned, organised and implemented. It is not difficult to draw complete assembly line. Steps can be taken to ensure the progress at each stage of work. It can be examined and checked whether development is adhering to the schedule. The only factor that cannot be made easily accountable is the role of manpower involved therein. Well, this factor can be handled tactfully. The output of each and every member of the industrial organisation can be judiciously defined. Our management techniques should be so developed that the differences between the production and productivity in an industrial organisation are eliminated or at least brought to the minimum.

It is high time that we increase our overall production to the extent it is possible and a movement to this effect is to be built up in our industrial world. If there is steady growth of trust, respect and love amongst the people, good results are expected. They should have mutual confidence and good faith. Our workers unions should not feel ashamed for raising the industrial output to the extent possible. Let us come out of the world of abstract debates and enter the phase of realisation. Here the irony is that if some leader dares speak the truth, he is hooted. The present tactics of the workers do not harm the industrialists alone, society suffers on the whole.

Future Leadership

Future leaders would not drive us to use 'Charkha' or even 'Sickle'. These are outmoded, since times have changed. Our people cannot be inspired to take historic steps with these symbols in their minds. Something new is to be cultivated. Coining of new slogans is also absolutely necessary. Fresh spirit is to be instilled amongst the people. They are to be in hurry. They cannot wait.

New Ideas

People expect that if new age is really dawning it should be based on those ideas that bear the support of their experiences. Gradually the respect for the names and ideas of Gandhi and Nehru would undergo a change.

We happen to live in a new situation which is extremely fragile. People have to know of their enormous potential and adjust with the mighty changes that are shaking the world.

Now it is time for reconstruction. New Movements are to take up the stock of present social, economic and political forces for their reintegration. Outside ideas and ideologies are to be scrutinised as to how far these can help us in attending to our problems judiciously. Bold and calculated steps are to be taken so that the energies of the masses could be collected from their depths and put on to some meaningful directions for pushing them out of their present state of pathetic existence. They would extend their cooperation only if they are convinced that possibilities of their exploitation have really been exterminated and they would receive more than their due. Now if they put in some additional labour, its fruits would not be eaten by others.

16

MOVEMENT (PART II)

"Man verily is sacrifice."

Chandogya Upnishad

"In accordance with the mass line, the majority, that is the intermediate and backward elements, must be taken care of, otherwise the advanced sections will become isolated and nothing can be done satisfactorily. The slogans of actions and the forms of struggle and of organisation we put forward before the masses must be acceptable to the intermediate and the backward elements. The development of self-consciousness and self-activity of the masses concerns chiefly with these people. A mass movement is possible only when these people are awakened and inspired to action . . . . . Our sole intention is to attract and to set in motion the intermediate and backward elements through active elements. In other words, it is for rallying the broadest possible masses that the active elements are to be organised. If the intermediate and backward masses are not yet awakened, we must know how to enlighten them as well as how to wait for them."

Liu Shao Chi

The first slogan of the new movement should be 'work for all" irrespective of the fact whether individual is skilled or unskilled or crippled or handicapped or even disabled. If he wills to work, it is to be provided. Here is a dilemma which cannot be overlooked. Some people have been provided with work. They agitate for better wages improved quality but lesser quantity of work. This is deplorable. Society suffers on this score. They know their rights and duties have never been brought home to them. Most of the trade union leaders believe that even references of responsibilities are signals of exploitation. Since rights are being over emphasized that is generating chaos all round. When our freedom movement was in full swing the question of reminding people about their duties other than those of agitations did not deserve attention, but thereafter also leadership did not set the record straight with the fear that people should not have felt it as suppression, something "new in old bottles". If we are really interested in ameliorating the lot of our entire society, some balance is to be struck between our rights and duties. The leaders have to pluck the courage to call spade, a spade.

New Food for Thinking

With the increasing complexities we find that problems of life are no longer revolving around social, economic and political realities only. These are undoubtedly important at their own places but there are other areas of life too, about which much is not debated. All India parties should acquire the services of a very large number of eminent psychologists, sociologists, anthropologists, cosmologists and others. They would form think thanks. There may then be great debates and discussions over the issues in which these specialists should participate and help out the parties in making use of scientific knowledge in developing their future policies. We must get out of our present times and ponder over what awaits us in the years to come. We are in need of discovering new areas that help in shaping positive attitudes of the people.

Leaders and their families

We get a very important hint from the ancient history of our land that the charge of a great movement should be taken over by those who have acquired a reasonable detachment in their day to day life. Those who are all absorbed in the affairs of their families, may, at time, fail to rise above their commitments to their relatives. Many things may creep in their lives which are not of any interest to the society. Many leaders of saintly background have failed and others who had responsibilities of their families did exceptionally well. Leaders succeed or fail for so many reasons.

Leaders

They should be able to prove to the followers beyond doubt that they have no personal axe to grind. If they have not come forward for the movement, they could have led a reasonably good life. They know the art of earning livelihood without dabbling in the affairs of the movement. Their commitment to the cause is founded on truth and some higher value system. A movement would spread quickly if the leaders and workers involved therein stand for certain principles that demand services and sacrifices more from them than from others who are likely to follow them. Use of tact and application of shrewd strategies by the leaders are important at their own place in social, cultural and political life, but these are no replacements for sacrifices and sufferings that the crusaders of a movement have to make. There is no dearth of unscrupulous elements amongst the people who are rabid opportunists. The real strength of a movement rests on the passionate thinking and sacrificing capacities of those who are leading it.

New Beginnings

It is the prerogative of every important generation to make certain beginnings that may endure. In the early stage it would appear as if the banner is being raised by some foolish, mad and sentimental idealists who have no understanding of hard realities. Their activities would soon fizzle out. Still there is something in their work that arrests the attention of the concerned. They appreciate devotion and commitment of those who are spearheading the movement. Once they are discovered, others also join their bandwagon. Gradually a new environment is created. Now more and more people follow the efforts being made and help the process of full construction. That is how the river of movement flows. Waves after waves come, storms rise and subside and by each such occasion history is created.

Past, Present & Future

The historians can take stock of the past events and present them in a fine logical and sketchy manner, as if that alone could have been the possible course available to those who were involved in the struggles. Events do not proceed in that cut and dry manner that we often read in the books. There are manyimportant details which are not given due attention and are soon forgotten. Historians have their viewpoints and handle only those events and incidents which may fit in their scheme of things. They are found snubbing even those who had played their part with the best of their ability but were ultimately found wrong as the times had marched on.

It is a formidable task to seize the spirit of one's own times and then act sagaciously. It is just like appearing at a tough examination whose results are to be declared later on. By then, it would be all forgotton as to what amount of efforts was put in by the examinees. Those who are in the thick of struggles are not very sure whether they have enough of information at their disposal on the basis of which they have chalked out their course of action. Still they act. They do not wait. They have set their goals. They have prescribed their policies. They have stated the paths they are following. They operate in the present with their eyes on future. A futurologist can, however, indulge in romantic exercises. It is not possible for those who are concerned with nation building activities.

Our Times

Real efforts can be made only in the present. We can neither transport ourselves to the past nor to the future for doing something important. Well, those who do not act in the present and quietly postpone everything to future would neither commit the mistakes nor go wrong anywhere. They have left no records of their performance. Most of our people prefer this simple formula of life. They wish to come and go unseen, unnoticed and unwatched. If they had not seen the light of the day and the darkness of night, the phenomenon of life would have continued as usual. Those who are involved in struggles would either fail or succeed. Result has its own importance and we cannot underestimate it. Even if we fail and that would not lead us far. The quality of our efforts put in the struggle might not have been appreciated by others, but we have the satisfaction of playing our role well. It is a great thing.

Important Question

Here is a principal question as to where and how should we begin our efforts for raising a movement. Would it do if we just try to prick a few bubbles on the surface of the society and then wait ? These are, namely the oppression of the capitalists in the industries ? The tyranny of the landlords in the countryside ? Fair price for food grains and industrial goods ? Attack on the economic disparities ? Atrocities on the women ? Wastage of working hours in factories and Offices ? Meaningless Dharnas ? Thoughtless strikes in industries ? The defects of present system of education ? Mal-administration of the hospitals ? Injustice through courts of law ? War against unemployment ? Rampant social evils ? Dowry system ? Burning of Brides ? Increasing corruption ? Failing law and order ? Lot of slum dwellers ? And what more ? And this list of the problems is not exhaustive.

Society

The society as we find it to day is suffering from so many ills. Its health would not improve through some magic touch of popular ideologies and philosophies. Suitable remedies of the major problems are to be found suggested, propagated, indoctrinated and executed. Then a chain reaction would start. One activity would leave its impact on other sides of life. The graphs of progress and development being shown by the rulers and the state agencies would please only those who are academically interested in the issues. Common people have their own barometers. They believe themselves to be the centre of universe and look at things accordingly.

I cry for those for whom nobody has ever shed a tear. More objective studies are to be made for our difficult conditions. All this statistics being made available is of little importance to those who live under the permanent shadows of hunger and starvation. The present spectacles of our academic and research studies are not correct. More genuine methods and better techniques are to be evolved. Only then a dispasionate examination of our socio-economic problems is possible.

Where steps are to be taken to increase production of those items which are consumed by the common people their prices should not be prohibitive? These should reach them at the minimum possible prices. In pursuit of quantity their quality should not also be adversely affected. Leadership of the movement is to be in a position to ensure that programmes are executed. There is something in the deep psychology of all unscrupulous men and women that they would not permit others to come in the domain of decent living. If good number of people could live well by working hard, the evil forces would feel handicapped. Their strength would reduce further.

Pioneers

The pioneers of future movements shall have to know and know it well that the human material they have to help is extremely difficult. It is more critical, more arguing, more non-cooperative and at the same time more agitating and all demanding. Still they shall have to play all calm and cool and collected. They have to work for seeking no regards, no rewards. Over it the task cannot be undertaken half heartedly since people in general are very fond of seeking quick results especially by doing nothing useful. The road is hazardous. Possibilities of failure are many. Still it is to be tried. There is no other choice. All these men and women around that we see are not just one piece. Each and every individual amongst them has so many things to know and do. We should not try to generalise about them. They are neither shadows nor mindless creatures. At times they are very tricky. We need not try to divide them vertically or horizontally. There are quite a few amongst them, may be in their soiled clothes, who are intelligent and see through things. They would stand by those who rise to the occasion. They are capable to become the "hardware" of the future society.

To begin with the founders of a movement should locate a particular group of the poverty stricken people, say of a particular area. They are apparently ill fed, ill clad, illiterate and badly housed. They have no adequate means of moderate living. Still they are men and women. They cannot be treated causally. Each one amongst them holds the opinion that he is important. He matters. At least he matters for himself and for those who are related to him. This is an example of working at micro level. This is to be expanded with all caution.

People are not just simpletons who can be led away. They hold strong religious and social beliefs, strong attitudes, a few other peculiar traits, some strange habits and what not. So many contradictory things are reconciled in the present state of their personalities, and they are carrying on the journeys of their lives. Most of them have many conflicts and tensions within themselves, but they know how to live with them. They ask questions to themselves and get replies from their depths. They do not abandon even those norms and practices which are choking the wheels of their lives and force them to languish in their miseries andthe present state of darkness. If effort is made that they should do away with them, that would hit their deeper depths where new thinking is still to acquire some foothold. If something is enforced by law, they reject, a "clear interference in their personal lives" according to them.

All this need not dishearten those who are coming forward to do something. This is the situation which they have to confront. The human material lying in misery is in fact unaware as to how far its thought constructs are chaining it to destitution. It is aligned with its own suppression. It would respond very slowly in the initial stages, but once movement picks up, it may move mountains.

Political Parties

Most of the political parties may not like to do much since their objectives are limited. Their activities revolve around politics and economics. Their ambitions are set. They have neither will nor ability to grapple with the civilisational crisis through which we are passing along with the other peoples of the world. Their major objective is to capture political power and then to hold it on. Every thing else is inconsequential to them. Their campaigns are for collecting of funds, throwing up catchy slogans, unfurling of party flags, organising meetings for collecting votes. participating in seminars, meeting press offering Satyagraha and so on. All this cannot transform a society like that of India.

Nature has its role to play. Each generation throws up its own crop of devoted and brilliant young men and women who wish that something more is done. They have a range of their own ambitions but they are scattered all over the country. They have no platform to ventilate their minds. They are to be located, persuaded and collected at one stage. Who would do that ? Obviously a new all India Party may take up thls responsibility. It should be founded on such a programme that is multi-dimensional. If possible the search of brilliant young man and women may be made through competitive tests and other selection methods. They would not come forward of their own to offer their services since they have no interests in political activities that are at work. If the arrangements are made to provide them bare minimum, their idealism may excite them even today to plunge in the movement. At the outset, they may appear to be weightless, but it would be soon realised that it is only they who understand the intricate dynamics of the society. Such people cannot be elected to assemblies and to Parliament since they have no funds for dabbling in politics which has been polluted beyond all description. It is now a prerogative of those few who are all rich. They have become political weight. How would they permit the campaign of honesty and integrity in the political life of the country ? If the well meaning bright young man and women could be roped in politics, they would put forth more constructive thoughts and bring better technique of implementation.

New order would not dawn of its own, it is to be created by our efforts. Causes to fight for are not likely to exhaust. Their number may perhaps increase with the passage of time. As soon as a few objectives are realised, many tensions may be eased. We shall come to realise many other problems which had been there but somehow that did not engage our attention.

Violence

In a civilised society, violence should not be permitted to

settle issues. It does not help much but damages the conditions beyond all repairs. There is not much of distinction between the victors and the vanquished afterwards. Even the causes of war are forgotten. Wounds remain as memory. The peaceful struggles for just causes are to be intensified, but at the same time, thereats of violence would be posed by those who would not like the caravan of the oppressed and downtrodden to move forward. The vested interests are there and their defenders would not permit others should assert and demand justice and fair play.

Crusader's lives are meant for a cause. If violence is thrust by the forces of conservatism, fanaticism, backwardness and other evils it is to be confronted valiantly. Defending of a great ideal generates a profound strength in the minds of the individuals. They would face all the agents of violence with courage and determination. Essentially they are the corps of peace and construction. While struggling they must ensure that all possibilities of proceeding peacefully have been exhausted. Their major concernment is to transform the minds of the people. They are to be warmed up for undertaking mighty tasks.

Finally comes the Question of the questions. Who would launch the movement ? Would it be a feat of one man or more ? Who would be such crusaders ? How shall we test it that they would hold the promise ? That would be a microscopic minority, a quiet band of miniprophets. They would not charge much of the price for their work. They are to give an undertaking that nothing would be demanded in return for sufferings and sacrifices borne. No war heroes. No political sufferers. They shall transcend. They are imbued with higher principles of life. They may drink from the springs of some religion or say some ideology or philosophy, or it may be some other source of deeper motivation, that would discipline their minds in a pattern and gradually they would ride over the crest of the waves.

17

WHITHER INDIA? (PART I)

"The human race had the wisdom to create science and art, why should it not be able to create a world of justice, brotherliness and peace? The human race has produced Plato, Homer, Shakespeare, and Hugo, Michelangelo and Beethoven, Pascal and Newton all these human heroes whose genius is only the contact with the fundamental truths, with the innermost essence of the universe. Why then should the same race not produce those leader capable of leading it those forms of communal life which are closest to the lives and the harmony of the universe?"

Leon Blum

This is the predicament. India is no exception. She is also one of the many countries of the world that form the United Nations today. She has, of course, marched on over these years but not in accordance with the aspirations of her founding fathers. They had set certain ideals like those of mountain peaks, "standing in all their majesty of sublime beauty". Thanks to them for the vistas they cleared, procedures they laid, efforts they made and the bit of will to fight they had tried to infuse amongst the people. Still fact remains. Leon Blum is correct in his assertion that ideal form of communal life has still not been raised by the mankind in any part of the world.

India is shaping in her own way. She is not following the proposed direction. We are not simply witnessing it rather playing our role in the manner we are capable. With the advent of political Independence in the year 1947, a new era was, of course, destined to dawn. State so emerged had taken over many of the functions relating to the reconstruction of New India but the people had quietly withdrawn to themselves though the ruling agencies were loudly claiming that they were of the people by the people, for the people. The truth had been not so. Whatever had been the character and efficiency of the Rule, people were found not much involved in many of its activities, although proclamations are made time and again that "we, the people of India" are doing. They are not looking up. Indifference is writ large on their faces.

What does not progress, obviousy begins to degenerate in due course. So over the years all great ideas of conceptual and ideological knowledge were left to stagnate and then decay. Many centuries old traditions and customs that were just placed under the carpet by certain great social and political minds of freedom struggle quietly came out for impressing upon the people to emulate the old backwardness. Who are doing this ? People. Why are they doing ? They have nothing else to do. After all they have to do something. It appears as if they have lost the direction.

Masses

Except for a small minority, our masses have been living in the ageless darkness. They do not know as to how history in their case is unfolding. Let us honestly confess what to say of man in the street, even those who stand on his shoulders and claim themselves to be educated and better placed have failed to demonstrate the required quantum of fidelity, cohesiveness, tenacity, heroism, conscience, inventiveness, and vigour. Here we cannot forget the valuable advice of Late Dr. Radhakrishan : "The future therefore depends on how we work, how we tackle this task". It is no use blaming some body at the top or at the bottom. It is easier to malign others but I look within myself and ask what is my contribution. What am I doing ? I feel ashamed.

New Raj

Leave aside, those lucky few who had once aligned themselves with the British Raj. They were amply rewarded and benefited under the foreign rule and most of their successors are noticed rolling in luxurious conditions even today. They had readily accepted the authority of new rulers of India after independence in the year 1947. They could so play their cards that new leadership could not help placing them on higher advisory positions in bureaucracy. So new India Raj was more or less in the hands of these lackeys of the British imperialism. Gradually certain changes were to begin, but the efforts of these so-called advisers were that a small group closer to the leadership should be fostered. So the beneficiaries of the new Rule were the relatives and friends of the leaders of the National Movement. A class of IAS men and women were trained for the perpetuation of prevailing order. It is very much in force.

That was not the objective of the freedom movement. So far people had been concerned, they were shown that many plans and programmes were being drawn up for their upliftment but nothing seriously was executed. As a result, even today they are ill fed, ill clad and badly housed in slums. Many of them are living on the pavements of our cities. Leaders talk tall of progress and advancement. Why is not being acknowledged by the people ? The truth is that our rulers are not in touch with the hard realities of life. Correct picture of the existing conditions does not reach them. The Bureaucracy cook up data and that is all.

After, all, what are the demands of poor people ? They do not ask much but just some clean water, a bit of fresh air, simple food, ordinary clothes, moderate medical aid, one room houses, simple schools for their children etc. Civilisation is advancing but these poor are languishing in the same manner as before. Why should they be denied even the bare minimum ?

Let us get out of urban centres and see the real quality of human life in the interior of the country. There is no water, no food, no clothes, all denials and deprivations. When the crusaders amongst them would arise for grappling with the problems, the new society with new concepts of "Property Relations" would obviously see the light of the day. The time is not far for such epochal changes.

Whatever we have experienced in the recent human history so far has been terribly painful. Even if light has spread, darkness has not reduced. Riches and luxuries have increased, but poverty and hunger have not decreased in the same proportion. Much is to be done on this front. It is doubtful whether present rulers are really seized with the magnitude of the tasks we are to face.

New Winds

By and large, people in the countryside have not increased their expectations since much did not reach them so far but at the same time it must be remembered that they know things are changing very fast. The rich are growing richer and even richest. The poor have fairly reasonable understanding of developing contours of modern life.

They know that there is something like standard of living. They have some minimum rights as well· They do not expect much and may be satisfied with modest living. Some immediate steps should be taken in this respect otherwise it may be too late. How would our nation builders propose to help them out ? Failure of those institutions that were required to deliver the goods is known to all around.

In our Eastern thought and culture, the responsibilities of the individual are overemphasized. Onus falls on him to become a good individual and with that over all society would be transformed. He upholds the banner of non-violence. That obviously results in atmosphere of peace and tolerance. All this does not help him for sharing gains but it helps the rulers alright to remain indifferent towards the people.

In our times conditions have changed. Central point is now society and the focus has been set on the performance of the state. Complexities of life have so multiplied over these few decades that individual dependence on the agencies of society and state has enormously increased. His contribution is acknowledged as if he is a part of a big machine. He cannot help it.

Modern History

Before J. L. Nehru and M.N. Roy had emerged on the political firmament of India, our freedom movement was led by those who had strong religious convictions. So far M.N. Roy is concerned, he was a great thinker who played most of his political innings outside the country. Nehru had always worked in close cooperation with Gandhiji. The latter was more a reality for the former than Gandhism, Nehru had all regards for Gandhiji's personality but not beyond that. This had proved a decisive break of the Indian polity with the religious past. We are still passing through an era in which this change over is gradually shaping new attitudes. The religious influences are slowly suffering decline.

There are certain theorists of our times who get support from Marxism as well as from other modern ideologies and impress that religion had always played a negative role in the human history. It is not our contention either that it had been a constructive and healthy force all the time. In the words of Winston Churchill, even "a golden model has a dark shadow". Our great leaders like Vivekananda, Tilak, Aurobindo, Gandhi, Maulana Azad and many others who led the national movement were strong religious minds. They sincerely believed that spirit of religion could have been used as a creative force for inspiring people againgst the British Imperialism as well as for raising Indian Nationalism.

They all propagated that by jointly participating in the Independence movement, the different religious communities would forget their petty differences. Their divisive tendencies would be blunted for building a united and free India. History goes in its own way. The part played by certain leading personalities and strange options accepted by a sizable section of one community during the struggle, dislocated everything. Many well meaning ideas of the national leadership were put to difficult tests. Credit may be given to Indian people in general that they did not abandon them. Prof. Ravinder Kumar has correctly put it, "If the political strategy adopted by Gandhi was a calculated risk, then it failed in one of its major objectives, namely the fusion of different religious communities into a distinct nation just as it succeeded in its other major objective, namely the liberation of India from alien rule".

Ideas and ideals

Now over forty years, we have been toying with different schools of ideas under the political concepts of namely Democracy, Secularism, Capitalism, Socialism, Democratic Socialism, Comm·nism, and so on. At present, we have so many brands of Capitalism, Socialism and Communism all available around. Each of these had left their marks on our psyche, but as ill luck would have it, all this had led us nowhere. Instead of explaining, and suggesting suitable solutions to our problems in the best possible manner, these have provided us a number of slogans, some formulas and a few impossible programmes. The issues have rather been confused and we are facing an opaque wall at the moment. We were crying against hunger and starvation, now we pray for adequate water supply. Other things would fallow. We cannot see through things at the moment. We do not know how to proceed further and wait as "lost children" in the "Fair of Life". Country is too big and leadership is not well equipped. Countrymen are too small in purpose though very large in number. They were never inspired to achieve the proposed goals. Whatever little progress has been made, it is nothing more than window dressing. The future historians would speak very low of our performance.

Nationalism

This is, in brief the millieu in which we people are living. It may be recalled that a decision was arrived at in the evening of the nineteeth century that Indianness should have been made a cause to provide the psychic security to the people as against phenomenon of caste, creed and religion, The principal objective was to struggle against the foreign rule but not to found a monolithic society or State. There were other ideals too since this had been a critical period of our history when new India was experiencing birth pangs before her brith. People should have come out of the confines of their narrow loyalties and set their focus on somthing higher. Leaders of those times had enriched the ideology of Nationalism with many ideas of sentimental practicality. For doing this, they had sought strength from the old faiths that were prevailing all over the country. They were at times influenced by the Western concept also.

All this was to cultivate a new spirit of self-respect, a pride in the past, and a belief in the future aligned with patriotism, meaning thereby to live and die for the country and for countrymen irrespective of their caste, creed, religion and place of birth in the country. History did not abide by the wishes of those who were championing the cause of such Indianness. The foreign rulers could have remained in power for a longer time through dividing people on so many scores. The rulers had given maximum attention to the communal forces against the rising tides of Indian Nationalism for so many decades and that finally led to the "surgical operation" of India.

18

WHITHER INDIA? (PART II)

Impact of Unplanned Urbanisation

"By 2000, most of the largest urban agglomerations will be in the third world, and half the third world population will be urban. In almost all third world cities, lower income groups lack space, drinking water, sanitation, waste collection, drainage, lighting, other urban services, minimally adequate housing, and even the acknowledged right to be where they are. Morbidity and mortality rates among the urban poor often exceed rates in rural areas. Compounding these problems are largely uncontrolled industrial and vehicular emissions. The magnitude of the problem has not been widely recognised nor given the sense of urgency it deserves".

Robert Repetto

Communalism has not been wiped out so far from our soil till date. Casteism is a social reality even today. Forces supporting regionalism have been strengthened over the years after independence. Their political influences are prominent in the scheme of our present democratic set up. Our election campaigners are subservient to all these factors which have not permitted our society to consolidate itself. Secularism and Indianness live on the lips of the few educated people who form a microscopic minority, but heads and hearts of those who matter are responsive to Communalism, Casteism and Regionalism.

Son of the Soil

The idas of the 'son of the soil' has acquired unusual importance over the years. Linguistic differences have become more pronounced than ever before. What does this certify ? People are doubtful about the vitality of nationalism as a force for providing them enough of confidence and security. Average men and women are always in need of certain props for their emotional survival. Only highly competent people, say doctors, engineers, managers, teachers, journalists, writers can depend upon their own potential. Under odd cricumstances even they are not in a position to protect their identities.

Many who claimed themselves to be all nationalists under the British Raj were put to all kinds of hardhsips there. With the advent of independence they became the centres of political powers and were committed to look after the interests of all who were lying oppressed. Things have not changed for the latter till date. They are nowhere. What could they do in the given circumstances ? They have kept themselves gummed with their past identities of castes and communities because these had struck them as all real and not mere abstractions. Caste is a powerful force in seeking petty middle level or even higher jobs and other benenfits from the state. Political position can also be had through it. What does the commitment to Nationalism provide at individual's level ? Nothing. So the people have remained settled in their traditional ways of thoughts. There has been no stirrings, and no upheavals in their minds. They are committed to their time old loyalties and seek comfort and strength from them.

India is too big a country. The task of seizing political independence was achieved and for that to think in terms of national interests was inevitable. Thereafter the necessity of all commitment to the same ideal was to be emphasized for achieving those lofty objectives that were promised in the freedom movement. Holding on to power was no objective. Country is still awaiting social, economic, cultural and spiritual revolutions and for that we need enormous efforts to put in. For achieving these epochal tasks a positive humanistic and broad conceptualisation of nationalism as an ideal is once again a necessity. It is also important to note we have to safeguard our freedom from external as well as from internal threats. As an ideology it should also encourage our mindfulness, expand our wisdom and generate wider human sympathies amongst our people for the world outside. The incubation of new ideas is a time consuming process. Let us start working on it with no loss of notice.

Urbanisation

Gandhiji was all against the phenomenon of urbanisation since his philosophy of life did not fit therein. Here he was trying to fight for a "lost cause" and so he stood defeated. Human race had been directed to urbanisation at a terrific speed over the recent years. This is a mighty civilisational change. We are destined to live with it and it is therefore imperative that we should adjust ourselves with its long term effects. We have no choice.

The first major problem created by it, is the increased sense of rootlessness amongst the people who migrate. This is a serious change which is to be given a suitable direction otherwise its side effects are perilous. It is to be treated as a challenge and converted into an opportunity. It depends upon the men to men and women to women as to how they receive it. Under its influence they are in a position to acquire a new perspective and thereupon work out fresh priorities. The intelligent amongst them would outsmart others and quickly adjust with the new situations. They feel no hesitation in adopting new professions. They watch as to how some people are progressing. They learn and imitate accordingly. With this their inertia disappears. Many backward looking ideas are abandoned by them. They shed fears of their insecurity also and thus become a new human kind. They join the race to conquer the world for the personal benefits. In their efforts all the rest is forgotton. There are many who fail to rise to the new situations and are found in miserable state in the urban world.

City life has its own hazards. Here everybody is self centred. As a result, he cannot think in terms of enchancing welfare of his street or market or offices. Empty drums are of course beaten. Programmes are drawn. Plans are prepared.

Meetings are held. Pamphlets and books are written. Resolutions are passed, but unfortunately their executions are never undertaken.

The city dwellers may be against the rich few who happen to be at the helm of affairs but they have no love lost for those who belong to their own economic strata and are below it. This is the tragedy of modern life. The conditions in the cities are growing terribly hopeless and people settled there reason out their ideas in such a manner as if selfishness is a cardinal virtue which should be adhered to under all stresses and strains. It is argued as if it strengthens competitive spirit and helps to browbeat equals. It is explained as a human reality which cannot be set aside. It is also defended as a "Principle" for upholding the banner of privacy. So they are its champions. It is put up as a solemn "right" above all susceptibilities. They fail to realise the far reaching consequences of their own thought processes and begin to decay in so many ways. In due course it appears as if they are no longer real men and woman of flesh, and blood. They are just shadows, all faceless and mindless. That is why there is far less civic sense in our cities than we find it in the villages and small towns.

If X is unconcerned with Y, why should latter bother about former ? Self centredness is no virtue. If the individual is all for himself, who would come to his rescue ? These inhabitants of the cities are a strange class of people who always desire that Gandhis and Nehrus should be born, but in the families of others. They may of course remain entitled for hoarding and expanding their own interests in all seasons.

The city dwellers of course work a bit more than their counterparts in the countryside, but they are very adept in swindling money. As they grow rich, they wish to become richer and even the richest. Here they set no limits on their ambitions. There are people in the cities who do not know what to do with the they money possess but still they are mad to increase it further. It is a matter of belief with them that with more money their esteem amongst relatives and friends would rise. They would become "illustrious" examples who should be followed.

There is a cut throat competition amongst the citizens. All

foul means are applied by them for climbing up quickly. So long as people were living in the rural side, they had some element of ethics cambined with so many taboos. The movement from the village to the city has changed the very basis of their living. As years pass by, they may occasionally go back to their villages and where they may hear some saner voice, but that is brushed aside since it appears to them something foolish or irrelevant or too idealistic and hence impractical. After generation or so their contacts with the rural world are almost snapped.

In this upheaval, we have discussed about those who amass wealth, whereas there are others millions and millions who have migrated to the cities but have failed to break the chains of their poverty. To some extent, their problem of hunger may have been sorted out, otherwise their overall quality of life as compared with that in countryside gets further depraved beyond all description. This de-humanisation of the urban poor is horrible to portray.

Middle Classes

Along with the few rich and many poor, there are many layers of middle class population in the cities. Most of the so-called educated people in the cities belong to this class. They face the biting realities of life which they are destined to live. They look up and try to vie with the rich in their conduct but the latter spite at them as emerging rivals.

The better awareness of the problems is incidently the prerogative of the middle classes and that makes them atonce more ambitious plus miserable. In their efforts, they may tire or fail or succed or even reach the top. All these possibilities are there in the womb of the circumstances. It has generally been noticed that if people from the middle classes fail to realise their objectives they turn angry and volatile and join agitational politics. Here is an opportunity for them to become petty leaders. Many of our present day middle level leaders in different opposition political parties hail from this very background.

In the cities, people are not religious in the sense we find them in the countryside. After moving to the towns they may adhere to their identities of belonging to a particular religious community or caste or place of their belonging. They assert the same too wherever it is considered necessary. Here unfortunately religions and castes get politicised. They acquire different dimensions.

In the cities people listen to radio, watch T.V., see films, and read newspapers and magazines. So their knowledge of political, economic, social and other affairs of life is more, but their understanding of the problems continues to be limited and parochial. Intellectual breakthrough of the people is a rare phenomenon. They seldom get opportunities to improve the horizons of their knowledge. Their perceptions may get politicised but emotional attachment with their traditional sense of belonging to a particular religion or caste or region remains unaffected. They fail to go beyond the past shadows of their beliefs for a long time. If somehow they are persuaded to scrutinise the positions they hold, they would certainly transcend and come closer to better understanding of things around.

The people living in the cities well realise that they are helpless and insignificant since they see that there are many like them. They are not engaged in some kind of stupendous tasks. They have come on this earth and would go away some day without making any remarkable dent. State and its agencies are omnipotent. That at times leaves damaging effect on their minds. The overall situation is so rotten that a common man in the city feels as if he has no weight, no prestige and no respect. We come across many well meaning and effective citizens holding commanding positions in their respective professions, but they are also found suffering from inferiority complex of some sort. They feel aggrieved to mention that they have been entrusted very important duties to discharge by their organisations but the society is all indifferent to them. Senior physicians, advocates, managers, administrators and many others complain that they do not hold deserving positions in cities like Delhi or Bombay or Calcutta.

Individual

If a city is a big machine, the individual is a very small cog in it. He is subservient to his wrist watch, or say to the siren of his factory. His supply of water, electricity, transport etc are controlled by the State. It provides him fuel, rationed food, medical facilities and even schools for his children. It is concerned with his milk supply and housing. What is the position of an individual in such an enlarged system ?

He is simply capable or qualified for doing something very small. If his necessities are well met through his earnings and he is in a position to survive, he carries on quietly. On the other hand, if his requirements are not being attended to, he believes others are out to destroy him. State is a party to it. That leads to his alienation. There are many who feel intensely disturbed on this score. They wish to take up the cudgels against this "alienations. They float parties, associations, institutions, and so on for fighting out against this disease, but their efforts more or less end in fiasco. The individual is therefore "a square peg in the round hole".

Urban vs. Rural People

It has already been pointed out that the urbanised people are more informed, more articulate, more argumentative, better dressed, than those who happen to live in the villages. Many facilities are provided to the former. Still all these plus points do not make them superior as individuals.

They are more absorbed in their personal needs. They do not love others and therefore they are not loved too. Most of them are bores, They are living machines otherwise "man" in them was killed long time back. They have no forward looking ideas. Their creative powers have dried up. Slightly better outside living is no proof of their better inside lives. The rural folk are more innocent. Their outside living may appear to be depressing, but they are at ease inside. The springs of love still flows from their minds. They are concerned with others around. They love their cattle and other domestic animals. They tend their plants and trees as if they are integral part of their total lives. They are more sensitive and affectionate. Perhaps their overall understanding of life is more deep.

Over centuries they have led lives of economic and social denials but that has not decimated them. Obviously they are not easily incapacitated by the terrible blows of lives which fall in the ways of all men and women from time to time. They demonstrate more of resilience and even endurance. We do not mean to glorify their lives but these few virtues are the remnants of their past otherwise we have shocking details of their overall living in recent times.

People are essentially immobile. They do not leave their homes and hearts for becoming opulents in the cities. Survival is the main point. There are two categories of migrants. The first one is of those who are professionally skilled and qualified, They cannot be suitably absorbed in the rural world. Their number is very small. The second category is of the waves after waves of human beings who are poor, unskilled and ever moving to the cities. It is damned hunger which comples them to invade cities. They come as uninvited guests and float in the civic oceans of miseries.

Townships

The best course for the increasing population is to live in small townships. These would be the ideal centres where the virtues of urban living can be integrated with those of rural life. Here pollution of environment would remain within control. The admission of the children to the schools would be feasible. The hospitals would also be reasonably neat and clean. Housing would not be an invincible problem. In short the depravity of human mind would remain in check. The people would not be in hurry. Their minds would get modernised to a considerable degree with out losing their emotional stability.

The promoters of big cities advocate the expansion of their cities till further. They argue that it would hasten the process of industrialisation and that is the need of the hour. All material resources, knowhow, finance, power, labour, transport and other things that help the industries to grow up quickly can be easily and rapidly procured in the big cities. Such possibilities do not exist at smaller places.

On the other hand, the controllers of the Government bodies of the big cities are found complaining against the unchecked growth of population. They cannot maintain adequate supply of electricity or of water or of housing and other things of the kind. After all there is a limit to which they can combat the situation.

Political Parties

All political parties are in need of such men and women who have qualities of "head and heart". They are more available in the cities. If a petty post of a peon or of a clerk is to be filled up in some public or private organisation, candidates have to pass through so many written, oral and medical tests, but for achieving political leadership in our country, there are no difficulties whatsoever. Of late the number of upstarts in politics has considerably increased in our cities.

There are no brilliant educated young men and women in the parties who are fired with imagination of building up a mighty India. Instead of wasting their resources in useless political activities, the leadership should apply its mind for raising cadres of task forces to execute those parts of their programmes which could possibly be undertaken with the means at its command. Well, a party may share power or not its existence can still be felt by its performance especially in our cities.

19

WHITHER INDIA ? (PART III)

National and Foreign Affairs

"As a member of the Chinese nation, I feel honoured to be a citizen of the International community. I am a son of the Chinese people. I deeply love my motherland and her people. We Chinese have created a glorious and ancient civilisation. But we have also undergone manifold sufferings and hardships and waged unremitting struggles, paying dearly for them. Today we are conscientiously summing up our experience and in the context of stability and unity are devoting ourselves to building a civilisation which is both materially developed and socialist in spirit. Through our own creative labour, we will radically transform the backward aspects of our country so that, with an entirely new look, it will take its place in the front ranks of the nations of the world. Together with the people of other countries, we will push forward the just cause of human progress."

Deng Xiaoping

It is true that history is largely shaped by those who have been in power. All the resources are at their command. They can decide their utilisation in the manner they like and as stated in the programmes and other documents of their parties. Their own likes are also very important though it does not mean that they have an element of self-aggrandisement. Men like Nehru, Patel, Azad and others who formed the vanguard of our freedom movement under Gandhiji took over the political power in the year 1947 with all humility. The truth is that most of them did not expect that opportunity of sharing it would ever fall in their life time. They were all, in fact, agitators par excellence. So when they were sitting on the thrones they permitted opponents to continue agitations. They had been respectors of democratic spirit through and through. So under the new order Gandhian methods of proceeding on hunger strikes, going to jails, fasts unto death etc. had continued as means to fight for justice and fair play. That had gone a long way in keeping our politics less violent. Since the steam against the rule could get out not before turning a force of huge destruction.

Opposit:on

Instead of making bold suggestions and warnings to the rulers the opposition was driven to personal attacks against those who were at the helm of the affairs. People had all regards for the leaders of the national movement. So opposition failed to grow creatively in this land. The question of its acquiring unity is ruled out by the events. It is divided into numerous groups as the centres of empty anger or thoughtless adventurism. So its record of forty years is worse compared help those who had been in power. It has never thought of working consttructively. Its leaders had never thought of setting up centres of collecting information of specialised nature. They have no mancankats no Press, no research cells etc. They have seldom attracted bright men and women who could have built up organisation for executing programmes. They could never throw up national programmes which could have clicked with the people. The ruling party has also been an abstract organisation, only rulers had mattered there. Opposition has not that advantage.

New Partymen

The so-called leaders had always been afraid of other educated and bright young men and women. Who would like to dig his own grave ? The leaders wish to remain in power only. They would not indulge in those activities by which their authority gets threatened.

Sooner or later some people shall have to rise to the occasion and help the history to have a positive turn. This generation has to find out ways and means for involving our brilliant and enthusiastic young ones in the programmes of socio-economic, political, cultural and moral development of society. They seem to have walked out from these areas of life where important deliberations are to be made for the National Reconstruction. They do not wish to compete with those who happen to sit on the destiny of the age. They have forgotten their real possibilities and are quietly attending to their petty position of lesser significance. If this process is not reversed our future would remain bleak.

We have a situation that our revolution may sprout from the grassroots levels. If a good number of promising young men and women come forward to educate and indoctrinate millions and millions to realise their rights and duties in the present context, fortune of the Indian society would change. It is a question of involving those who are at the rock bottom. They are to be fired with constructive ideas.

Transport and Communication

Over the years, transport facilities have increased. People are now more mobile and are also travelling more than ever in the past. Their awareness of the world in which they happen to live is more than that of their parents. On the other hand, possibilities of launching false and mendacious propaganda by the unscrupulous elements have also increased beyond all proportions. That may adversely affect the people's perceptions and then their thought processes. The over all situation can be so twisted that even the so-called knowledgeable may get badly confused. Only right information can help in working out correct solutions of the problems. It is true we do not happen to live under idealistic conditions, but still fact remains that new consciousness about life around is growing.

Communal riots

Most of the communal riots are not just casual or rational or logical outbursts. These are carefully worked out and spread in which common people who are innocent in all respects are trapped. We may spread out in the villages, towns cities etc. and take thoughtful and suitable measures well in time that conditions do not get out of control. What has the formal education done in this respect ? It is not a simple task to persuade unruly mobs when their tempers are high. Members of task forces should be adequately motivated. Here is an area where many efforts are still to be made. Unfortunately we permit the atomosphere to vitiate and thereafter apply "Police Force" and then from "Peace Committees" i.e. after all the evil has been done.

Unity and Diversity

We hear too much of Unity and Diversity in our culture, thought and life. Mountains of data are there which can be tailored in defence of Unity against Diversity and vice versa. Many contradictions are well settled in our minds and we do not feel irked. If we try to put them together and ask ourselves how things are reconciled, we open the gates of confusion. Immediately after the independence in the year 1947 it was a matter of belief with those who mattered, that champions of diversity would be contained in view of building up a strong, united, secular and modern India. If the protagonists of diversity had raised some storm, that would be in the tea-cup. It was fondly hoped that the generation of "National Consciousness" would supercede many of the time-old loyalties. Unfortunately history has not moved accordingly. In our times it has become a very serious and sensitive issue and that occupies our attention forth with. Its inept handling may prove very disastrous.

Late Maulana Azad used to say that the defenders were available for even a useless cause. If divisive tendencies are permitted to grow stronger, there is no dearth of unscrupulous elements in the society who would always try to exploit the situation for destabilising the country. Some foreign powers would also come to help them by adding fuel to the fire.

In the circumstances, our stand on this basic issue should be unequivocal that "Unity" of the country is our first priority. No compromise is possible over this essential. India is an ancient land and so many languages are spoken here. So many religious communities are living here. So many civilisations and cultures have prospered and decayed here. History speaks for the rise and fall of so many kingdoms and empires. To cap it all, the climatic conditions, food habits and living styles of the people are not identical. Apparently all these considerations uphold the case for diversity, and it should be acknowledged in all fairness but not at the cost of National Unity. Languages and Cultures should grow and flourish within the national framework and not for Balkanising the country. This is a cruel world, we should support those ideas and forces by which the process of "Nation Building" is strengthened. If we remain divided in our minds or remain involved in those causes that affect National Unity we are doing great disservice to posterity. We are, of course, not for imposing some kind of uniformity. People shall have to ensure that the fabric of India as a nation is not weakened.

Nehru and Foreign Affairs

We have all regards for late Pandit Jawaharlal Nehru as a great leader of our land who played a notable part in the national movement and thereafter for building up a strong, democratic, modern and secular India. As a Prime Minister he was at the helm of the affairs for more than sixteen years till he passed away in the year 1964. It is fairly a long period for laying the foundations of new India. As a world statesman, he was the first great Indian who visulalised the importance of integrating India's freedom struggle with similar struggles and movements in other parts of the world.

It is as early as first decade of this century when Lord Curzon, then the Viceroy of India, recorded in his famous article "Problems of the Far East", "The Indian empire is in strategic centre of the third most important portion of the globe . . . . in the political influence which she exercises over the destinies of her neighbours near and far and the extent to which their future revolves upon Indian axis". Pandit Nehru was fully conscious as to what role India could play in shaping the destiny of Asia. He picked up the threads of the Indian Foreign Policy well in time in the third decade of this century. He wished India should have played her legitimate role in the future history. She should extend all possible support to those parts of the world that were languishing under the foreign imperialisms. In view of her long history and culture India was also to strive for peace and prosperity for the entire human race.

It was, however, well understood by Nehru in late fifties that Chinese were though Asians yet had different perceptions about future. Nehru stuck to his own designs. India had a mission to fight against Imperialism, Colonialism and Racialism. There has been consistency in her policies. She was not to emerge as a rival to China in the comity of the nations. Empire building could not have been an ambition of Indian leaders. Over the years, many countries of Asia, Africa and other parts of the world had been liberated and then they did not wish to forfeit their freedom by submitting again to some super power. So they preferred to defend freedom by their own efforts and plan future. They had that bit of common sense regarding international affairs, that others would not come to their rescue if they were in trouble. It is not the world of Buddha or of Christ. Thinking on these lines had given birth to the "Non-Alignment Movement" all over the world. India stands there at the moment. Credit must be given to Nehru, Mrs. Gandhi and others for evolving such a foreign policy of India. It reflects the touch of idealism which emanates from the history of this country.

20

WHITHER INDIA? (PART IV)

"Propaganda always has some policy. The policy probably will not be made by the propagandists, and it probably will not remain for ever the same. Since policy is the sequence of growing decisions in any body politic, it is likely to fluctuate through time as changing conditions alter issues and modify alternative. Although its policy may shift, however, the purpose of propaganda remains constant : to serve that policy with maximum effectiveness".

Daniel Lerner

Let us confess that the achievements of our government are not spectacular. We have to pick up the threads from here if people are to be involved in launching mighty movements. As and when we recall the excitement of our people for independence, i.e. prior to the year 1947, a peculiar sensation runs through our minds and bodies. Its simple and casual recall makes us feel as if we are proceeding on a pilgrimage to a particular era when so many great sons of the country were working together and pushing the people towards a set goal. They had strong ambitions to rebuild this country. Unfortunately this great responsibility was passed over to others including ourselves. The painful truth is that our generation had failed. It has not that yearning for reconstruction.

Leaders

Well, whatever was achieved or not achieved by Nehru and Mrs. Gandhi is a matter of the past. We cannot now transport ourselves to those years for recreating our socicty. We have to operate in our own "times and space". Instead of delving over their compulsion, we should try to know what is to be done now. They were not omnipotent nor are we.

It is, of course, true that they did not work much to strengthen their party. They were at the helm of the affairs and all elections were won by the Congress Party through their personalities. Party members were mere common people and as such they could not help looking towards their leaders for survival.

Why did not the leaders work for raising a strong and dynamic, social, economic and political force or a party or a movement ? It is still to be investigated. Ultimately all moons, all years, all days, all winds, all problems, all difficulties adopt their course and time passes away. So these leaders had come and gone. Even the present leadership would become a matter of the past with the passage of time. Still we hope it is capable to achieving some thing spectacular. Let us get out of our past and focus our thinking on present and future. It is our solemn duty to study the whole situation dispassionately and plan to work in view of our new assessment. All leaders have to work under so many pressures. Under all conditions they have to emphasize that the actions being taken by them would help the masses.

Our people in the rural side are living under pathetic conditions. On the national scale, there are no regular programmes to organise them in a such a manner through which feeling may be cultivated amongst them that they are a great people involved in certain epochal tasks. Only when fears of droughts and starvation loom large on the minds of those who hold the keys of the government the work begins. All programmes are abandoned as soon as the news of drought and famine become stale. It is believed that the anger of the people, has by now subsided. They would not raise voice.

This is no people's involvement in the national reconstruction. Let our MPs & MLAs think, go and work in their respective constituencies at least for a few years and inspire people to undertake a few voluntary tasks for building up certain projects namely roads, canals, schools, hospitals and so on. These efforts would help the nation materially. They must get them completed under their on guidance and supervision. That may ultimately determine leaders' potential and their contribution for promotions in the ranks of the party. We have no such norms. The law of jungle is prevailing in the market of politics. Many well-meaning, sincere, selfless and intelligent workers who at times join some party with strong sense of idealism are found indifferent and disgusted after some time. They quietly leave the field open to those who dabble in politics for seizing power only. Politics is their profession otherwise they are in no way better than average men and women. They have no capacity to renounce their personal advantages for the sake of others.

Masses are generally ignorant, less informed, scattered and unsystematic. The real task for the present and future leadership is to organise them and make them understand their responsibilities. We are, therefore, in search of those dcvoted young men and women who should have a sense of belonging to the masses and been prompted by their personal character to work for them. Their actions would then be flowing from deeper yearnings.

Many Heroes and Heroines

At the moment, there are very few spheres of our lives where people could have demonstrated their heroism. Our young children are in this impression that heroes and heroines are there only in the "Film World". Let us prepare detailed lists of those important activities which should be performed by the people. There are many heroes and heroines in agriculture, commerce, industries, education, science, technology, hospitals, armed forces, sports, literature and so on. In that case, many people would resolve to find their names in the Roll Call of Honour. That would cultivate right spirit of achieving some thing amongst large number of people

If there are a few peaks to climb, the number of climbers would not be very large. Let us propose many heights and show to the people for demonstrating their skills and strength. It would be in the fitness of things if the present government picks up this idea with all sincerity. At the moment this is being followed in the Armed Forces. Why should it not be extended to other areas ? Our intellectuals, litrary writers, social workers and others may be given due attention. The truth is that they are neglected. It is they who intensely feel the pulse of the people whether they are moving or not. They state the unexpressed desires of the teeming millions and even suggest suitable ways and means as to how people should "grapple with the problems".

Indian Communist Movement

With all our regards for Marx, Lenin, Stalin, Mao and many others, we cannot help saying that the Indian Communist Movement had not played plausible role in our modern history. It has never instinctively felt as a great Nationalist party. Most of its leaders have all along been finding faults in the Nationalist Movement and its leadership without throwing up any meaningful alternative which could have appealed to the people at large. Till date, its appeal is limited to certain areas and pockets. Under Gandhi and Nehru, Indian Nationalism had no aggressive designs and as great leaders of their times they were concerned with the poorest of the society.

On the world scene, Communist States are emphatically conceding the role of Nationalism in shaping and reshaping of their societies. "Socialism in one State" was a programme to be implemented by the Soviet Communist Party under Stalin. We have noticed how Chinese have been strengthening their "State apparatus" after their revolution in 1949.

The CPI & CP(M) and other Communist Parties that exist in India today pay no attention to the nationalistic aspirations of the people and lay emphasis on the ideological issues in such a manner as if Indianness is of no consequence. They have, in their thoughts and deeds, ignored the geunine national interests of their people either for pleasing some outside power or for certain other political gains. Late Romesh Thaper, an eminent journalist who was known for his leftist leanings had pointed out, "This superficial analysis and the obstinate refusal to correlate events, blinded the Communist party and prevented it from understanding the new emergent forces in the national situations".

Indian Socialists

The Indian socialists have also no admirable record. They were at once Socialists, Gandhians and what not. During freedom struggle they were fully aligned with the National Movement where distinctive contributions were made by them. Thereafter, they were found confused, and a badly divided lot of people. Most of them have been idealists and were disappointed as to how the country was proceeding under the captaincy of Nehru and Mrs. Gandhi. Instead of making some positive contribution in proposing what was conducive for the overall health of the country, they were found wasting their steam and energy in thoughtless criticism of the Congress leaders and their policies.

Nehru had his own compulsions. He could not speedily drive the country towards socialism since most of the eminent Congressmen were not for it. With the passage of time, the Indian Socialist Movement had lost its precise direction. Some of its leaders had joined Congress, others kept seating on the fence and the rest were satisfied with abusing and rebuking Congress Party without rhyme and reason.

Let us state here that Gandhiji was not a socialist. This is no adverse comment for the Father of Nation. For Gandhiji, "Self-Government means a continuous effort to be independent of government control whether it is foreign government or a national government. Swarajya Government will be a sorry affair if the people look up to it for the regulation of every detail of life. A nation that runs its affairs smoothly and effectively without much of state interference is truly democratic. Where such condition is absent, the form of government as democratic is only in name".

He had stated somewhere in more emphatic words, "I look upon increase in the power of the state with the greatest fear because although while apparently doing good by minimising exploitation it does the greatest harm by destroying the individuality which lies at the root of all progress". Very strangely many of Indian socialists who were well meaning patriots wished to remain ardent followers of Gandhism. A peculiar contradiction. In socialism it is always from above that planning begins and goes down. It hold that State is operating in the best interests of the people, and they should therefore, obey its commands. So the ideological position of the Indian socialists has been confused. They are of course Indians through an through. They uphold the banners of democracy and secularism.

Indian National Congress

So far as Congress is concerned, it has the privileged history. The support of almost all great Indians of modern times had been reserved for it. Right from its earliest years party had tried to assimilate many traits of "Indian life and culture". What is important to note is that even those great Indians who had never sought its actual membership but were patriots of great order had subsequently found honourable place in its history. If someone had angrily walked out of the party on some principle, he was accorded a deserving status. Sardar Bhagat Singh was not in the party but we find him affectionately being discussed in its history. Subhash Bose had left Congress in disgust but his patriotic spirit is recalled with gratitude by most of the Congressmen even today.

Right since the second decade of this century many great minds of India had joined Congress. Their dominance in the party as well as in the country was not questioned. That had been the real reason for which inner party debates were never encouraged in its functioning. Who could dare speak against the views expressed by Bal or Pal, or Lal or later on by Gandhi and then Nehru ? That legacy continues. Now those stalwarts who could have influenced history are no longer there but debating over intricate issues is still not permitted in the Congress Party, as there has been no tradition of it. A wrong and undemocratic practice was set up with good faith many years ago and that is being adhered to. Many well meaning Congressmen are found uneasy on this score but keeps mum on this score.

Our times are different. If some Congress leader may be of little consequence, has stuck to his view or it could just be an ego question, he resigns from the party and founds an other one with an all India nomenclature. The congress as it is, does not permit to contain him in the party. There are, as such, many all India parties with very little following of the people. They are the children of Congress claiming its inheritance.

It would be unfair on our part to say that all those who had left Congress from time to time were selfish or reactionaries. Congress had been a Bunyan tree of modern Indian history. Religious Gandhi and Azad, Radical Nehru, Socialist JP and Conservative Patel and Dr. Rajendra Prasad had all worked shoulder to shoulder in its fold. They all had well understood that in the larger national interests their personalities were not to clash. They had realised the importance of unity but this could not have been an all time affair in a political organisation. Times change. Political consensus could have easily been achievable under them and no great break up was possible in the presence of imposing personalities but it is not a correct practice.

If we dispassionately study as to how the national leadership had been conducting the affairs of the party, a high sense of disappointment seizes us since it did not help events to proceed logically. If in the process too much was saved and better results obtained, something had been lost too. Many streams of creative thoughts had not been allowed to flow. Many ideas were rejected without ever being considered. There were always efforts for adjustment, compromise, accommodation and so on. That is why the thinking of the Congress party could never be chiselled and pointed in its long history.

Present Congress

In our times there has been a definite change at all levels of party. It is no longer an organisation of selfless volunteers. Since party has been in power for the last forty years, many ambitious people have wrested positions in it. Selflessness is no longer a criterion for seeking importance. So the members are not required to demonstrate it. The new aspirants should have money, manpower and if possible muscle power. Tact is more important than intellect.

The leadership reminds the nation time and again that the notable part played by the party in the freedom movement should not be forgotten. That should remain a source of inspiration, but all this does not ring plausible to day. The truth is that there is nothing to emulate from the present day

Congressmen whatever may be their status in the party. Most of them are below average ability without commitment to the causes. They are professional politicians.

It is high time that it should induct new blood, efficient men and women who should possess sterling qualities of head and heart. They should understand their enormous responsibilities and meet the challenges with courage and conviction. They must know how to act intelligently with a strong sense of sacrifice whether in power or without it. Their records should prove that they have worked amongst the masses and have helped them in acquiring a better quality of living. "Life" according to the Gita, "is sacrifice".

Social Movement

We are in need of an epochal social, economic, political and spiritual movement which should involve our millions and millions. We may lay down such conditions that its membership would be opened to only those who have devoted at least a few years or so in doing serious social and political work. Let us not forget that rulers in democracy must be in a position to prove that they are well-behaved, sober, intelligent, daring, and well meaning. They ought to be ready to make supreme sacrifices for the causes dear to them. They are to set examples for others. They are not simply meant for sticking to high positions only. Corrupt and coward rulers bring discredit to themselves, insult to the parties and shame to their country.

Role of Party Press

Most of our all India Parties are failing on the front of propaganda. These should immediately launch a few all India weeklies, journals and other magazines in all the national lauguages. There is an old saying that journalism is the "fourth estate". The writing included in the party organs should highlight not what the government is doing rather what the parties would like it do. The correctness of this emphasis should be understood. There should be open debates on the important issues. This would help in generating healthy and mature public opinion. The views of the concerned would also be crystallised. If considered necessary, Party leaders may requisition the services of bold and intelligent journalists. A particular party is in power or not, it should always play a decisive role.

People had long felt secure under the Congress rule. They are quietly thinking as how it had failed as their organisation. The alternative is not in sight. People fear that their freedom is in peril. Still our investigations of deeper psychology confirm that they have feelings for Congress. They think, reflect, plan theories and conceptualise under its culture.

If it has to survive, it shall have to restrucuture its policies. Certain new values are to be injected. Instead of drawing the attention of the people to thepast the performance of those who are in power should be debated. Those who give their best should be supported, admired, awarded and rewarded. In the words of Dr. Radhakrishnan, "We lack nothing so far as the theoretical formulations and wise maxims are concerned, but in our practical application of these we fall behind".